Praise for *Wonderfully Made*

Allie Marie Smith's story is relatable, honest, messy, and filled with hope. She is a woman who has discovered the life-altering truth of who she is to Christ and in Christ. I'm so glad she has written this book to help other young women discover the beauty of this reality as well.

STASI ELDREDGE, *New York Times* bestselling coauthor of *Captivating: Unveiling the Mysteries of a Woman's Soul*

Our young women need leaders who love God, love grace, and are passionate about the identities that are ours for the taking. As a mom, as a woman, as an author, and as a fan of this next generation—I'm so grateful for Allie Marie Smith and this book. We need it! Our girls need it! I highly recommend picking it up for a gal in your life

JESS CONNOLLY, author of *You Are the Girl for the Job* and *Breaking Free from Body Shame*

Such a timely message! If you've ever struggled with insecurity or wished you could change parts of your story, Allie's words are for you. She's a wholehearted encourager, insightful guide, and an honest voice of hope that will lead you into true confidence and more of God's best for your life.

HOLLEY GERTH, bestselling author of *The Powerful Purpose of Introverts* and life coach

Wonderfully Made is a timeless and timely message that Allie has lived out so well in her own story and in community. This book is the beautiful fruit of her deep years of sowing and struggle, rooting and redemption.

KATHERINE WOLF, author of *Hope Heals and Suffer Strong*

When you need a dose of truth, when you need to hit the reset button on life, when you need someone to hold a mirror up to you and show you what God sees, this is the book for you. Thank you, Allie, for teaching us what it means to be wonderfully made with honesty, vulnerability, wisdom, and sincere sisterhood.

KATE MERRICK, author of *And Still She Laughs* and *Here, Now*

Allie has a heart to see hearts turn away from the mirror and put them back onto Jesus. *Wonderfully Made* is a reflection of just that! This book is a must-read to dive deeply into who God is and who you are in Him.

CAMBRIA JOY, author of *Growing Strong*

Wonderfully Made

DISCOVER THE IDENTITY, LOVE, AND WORTH YOU WERE CREATED FOR

ALLIE MARIE SMITH

MOODY PUBLISHERS
CHICAGO

All Scripture quotations, unless otherwise indicated, are taken from the Holy Bible, New International Version®, NIV®. Copyright © 1973, 1978, 1984, 2011 by Biblica, Inc.™ Used by permission of Zondervan. All rights reserved worldwide. www.zondervan.com The "NIV" and "New International Version" are trademarks registered in the United States Patent and Trademark Office by Biblica, Inc.™

Scripture quotations marked NLT are taken from the Holy Bible, New Living Translation, copyright ©1996, 2004, 2015 by Tyndale House Foundation. Used by permission of Tyndale House Publishers, a Division of Tyndale House Ministries, Carol Stream, Illinois 60188. All rights reserved.

Scripture quotations marked ESV are from the ESV® Bible (The Holy Bible, English Standard Version®), copyright © 2001 by Crossway, a publishing ministry of Good News Publishers. Used by permission. All rights reserved.

Scripture quotations marked NKJV are taken from the New King James Version. Copyright © 1982 by Thomas Nelson. Used by permission. All rights reserved.

Brief sections of this book were previously published on the author's blog and at darlingmagazine.org.

All emphasis in Scripture has been added.

Names and details of some stories have been changed to protect the privacy of individuals.

Published in association with the literary agency of WTA Media, LLC Franklin, Tennessee.

Edited by Amanda Cleary Eastep
Interior design: Ragont Design
Cover design by Derek Thornton / Notch Design
Cover image of pottery copyright © 2020 by Marco Montalti / Alamy Stock Photo (2E233BM).
Cover image of clay texture copyright © 2020 by komkrit Preechachanwate / Shutterstock (428415445).
Cover image of pottery texture copyright © 2020 by Declarations Images / Shutterstock (1466656031).
Cover image of ceramic texture copyright © 2020 by Nob2020 / Shutterstock (1835815378).
All rights reserved for the images above.
Author photo: Lena Fredrickson

Library of Congress Cataloging-in-Publication Data
Names: Smith, Allie Marie, 1983- author.
Title: Wonderfully made : discover the identity, love, and worth you were created for / Allie Marie Smith.
Description: Chicago : Moody Publishers, [2021] | Includes bibliographical references. | Summary: "Finding your value and purpose begins with a simple but profound truth: you have been wonderfully made. Don't believe the lie that your worth comes from your achievements or looks. No matter what others say, God declares that you are His creation and His eternal plan for you is good"-- Provided by publisher.
Identifiers: LCCN 2021026552 (print) | LCCN 2021026553 (ebook) | ISBN 9780802424365 | ISBN 9780802499967 (ebook)
Subjects: LCSH: Christian women--Religious life. | Identification (Religion)--Religious aspects--Christianity. | Women--Religious aspects--Christianity. | BISAC: RELIGION / Christian Living / Women's Interests | RELIGION / Christian Living / Inspirational
Classification: LCC BV4527 .S62195 2021 (print) | LCC BV4527 (ebook) | DDC 248.8/43--dc23
LC record available at https://lccn.loc.gov/2021026552
LC ebook record available at https://lccn.loc.gov/2021026553

Originally delivered by fleets of horse-drawn wagons, the affordable paperbacks from D. L. Moody's publishing house resourced the church and served everyday people. Now, after more than 125 years of publishing and ministry, Moody Publishers' mission remains the same—even if our delivery systems have changed a bit. For more information on other books (and resources) created from a biblical perspective, go to www.moodypublishers.com or write to:

Moody Publishers
820 N. LaSalle Boulevard
Chicago, IL 60610

1 3 5 7 9 10 8 6 4 2

Printed in the United States of America

To Paul, Mom, Dad, and Timmy—
Thank you for fighting for me when I couldn't fight for myself.

And to my three nieces: Addison, August, and Julia Marie—
May you come to know what it truly means
to be wonderfully made.

Contents

Introduction

Knowing the truth about who you are, why you are here, and what you've been made for is the key for living a whole-hearted life of freedom and purpose. It is the doorway through which you can heal from your deepest hurts and live into your full potential. When you recognize the source of your worth and identity, it changes everything and brings joy and purpose to your steps.

My journey toward discovering these truths has felt like a joyride through emerald forests and an unwanted detour through endless stretches of scorching desert . . . with a few flat tires along the way. I am still traveling through life alongside you, soaking in the splendor of it all, while unearthing the courage to face the hard parts I'd like to bypass. Each leg of my journey has made up the story of my life.

I got my first flat tire when I was eighteen driving alone to San Francisco in my blue Ford Explorer. Just weeks earlier, I had graced the stage at my high school graduation wearing my royal blue cap and gown with a smile stretched across my freckled face.

I was a girl who was working overtime to keep up. A good girl from a good home, I excelled in school and soccer and was a part of the popular crowd at my all-girls school.

With an acceptance from a top university waiting for me, it looked on the outside like I had it all together; but on the inside, I was coming apart. The sadness I had been keeping at bay since I was a twelve-year-old girl overtook me, and because of many complexities, I found myself in a dark clinical depression, unable to sleep, eat, or talk. My body was alive, but there was no life within me. My parents admitted me to the psychiatric hospital where I was put on antidepressants and sent home three days later.

On an overcast day that June, still gravely depressed, I grabbed my car keys, hopped in my Explorer, and took off with one destination in mind: the Golden Gate Bridge. Weaving through traffic and up winding city side streets, I felt numb and my mind raced as my golden-brown hair danced wildly in the wind. Suddenly, it appeared in the distance. The massive rusty, orange structure stretched across the skyline. I came with the intention to end my life by jumping off of it.

I was so sick I believed the lie that the world was better off without me in it. This was the only way I thought I could escape the pain. As I recklessly turned a corner, I heard a sudden, loud thump. I stopped the car to discover a flat tire. Paralyzed, I sat in my car unsure what to do. There was a knock on my window. A silver-haired man with a warm smile asked if he could help. I nodded my head yes, and he called for roadside assistance.

For several minutes, I engaged in a real conversation with that kind-hearted man. He had no idea where I was headed or what my intention was. After weeks of not talking, I felt less alone because of my conversation with him. It gave me hope that maybe I would be okay. After my tire was fixed, I turned around and headed home to my family.

During my second hospitalization that fall, after trying to start college on the East Coast, I began to read the Bible. One day I stumbled across Psalm 139 in which David, the psalmist, writes, "I praise you [God] because I am fearfully [lovingly] and wonderfully made." These words became an anthem over my life, pointing me to the source of my true value after depression told me I was not worthy of living.

My struggle with depression at the age of eighteen and again at twenty-one was excruciating. Though my life isn't perfect and I've had setbacks, I am now thriving, free from depression even though I live with a mental health condition.

I see my struggles as one of the greatest gifts in my life. They led me to a personal relationship with God, my source of life and hope. I am not ashamed of my past because I know my trials don't define me, but God's love for me does. Through my faith, professional help, and the support of my family, God has picked up the pieces of my life. He has mended them into something beautiful. God has given me a life more whole and purposeful than I ever could have imagined. I believe He can do this for you too.

Although my life isn't always easy, God has filled me with joy and purpose. I spend my days pursuing my passion of helping girls and young women know God and know their value through the ministry I founded. Many mornings, my husband Paul and I head to the beach for an early morning surf with our golden retriever Gidget in tow. Acting like a music director with one hand on the wheel and one hand directing me (his choir), he belts out bluegrass songs at the top of his lungs and I join in, always off tune, as the sun rises over the Pacific. My life is filled with beauty and adventure. After struggling so much in the darkness, I don't take a single day in the light for granted.

Whether you've had your own breakdowns or not, you know life can be hard. It is challenging to be a woman in this world. Some days, life can seem unbearable. We might question our worth or think our value is in our looks, accomplishments, and influence. At times, our days can feel overwhelming or directionless, and we might feel insignificant. We too easily can accept the toxic narrative our culture sells us. We often believe the lies in our head that tell us we're not good enough or worthy of love.

We are women in search of meaning, trying to make sense of the world. As we go about our lives, in the quietness of our own thoughts we ask:

Why am I here?

Does my life matter?

What is the purpose for my life?

Whether you've asked these questions on a mountaintop or on your way to the grocery store, they can't be ignored. They must be faced head-on with a brave heart. The conclusions we come to about these foundational questions matter. They shape the core of our being—our identity, sense of purpose, and value.

When we don't know who we really are or have a clear direction for our lives, we wander this world aimlessly . . . sometimes right into destruction. But God has given us a map that will guide us through detours, breakdowns, and flat tires as we are invited to journey on the road that leads to life. I hope this book, filled with eternal truths from the bestselling and most life-changing book of all time, the Bible, will guide you in your life. I hope that through it you will discover the identity, love, and worth you were created for.

Research has found that 87 percent of people believe in God; however, He has been pushed out of the world He created, and we are suffering because of it.[1] But we are not without hope, and a better life is waiting for us if we choose to receive it.

So, over the next thirty short chapters, I invite you to take a journey with me as we explore who God really is, who He created you to be, and thirty unique purposes you've been made for. Whether the truths contained in the first three chapters are new to you or not, they will build a strong foundation as you begin to fully step into your true identity and purpose. Whatever you believe about spirituality or faith, I hope you will open your heart and come with me as we explore what it really means to be wonderfully made. Consider inviting a friend. Or gather a small group of women to join you, and use the book club questions in the back to guide your discussion. Are you up for the adventure?

Love,

Allie

Psalm 139:1-18

You have searched me, LORD,
    and you know me.
You know when I sit and when I rise;
    you perceive my thoughts from afar.
You discern my going out and my lying down;
    you are familiar with all my ways.
Before a word is on my tongue
    you, LORD, know it completely.
You hem me in behind and before,
    and you lay your hand upon me.
Such knowledge is too wonderful for me,
    too lofty for me to attain.

Where can I go from your Spirit?
    Where can I flee from your presence?
If I go up to the heavens, you are there;
    if I make my bed in the depths, you are there.
If I rise on the wings of the dawn,
    if I settle on the far side of the sea,
even there your hand will guide me,
    your right hand will hold me fast.
If I say, "Surely the darkness will hide me
    and the light become night around me,"
even the darkness will not be dark to you;
    the night will shine like the day,
    for darkness is as light to you.

For you created my inmost being;
    you knit me together in my mother's womb.
I praise you because I am fearfully and wonderfully made;
    your works are wonderful,
      I know that full well.
My frame was not hidden from you
    when I was made in the secret place,
    when I was woven together in the depths of the earth.
Your eyes saw my unformed body;
    all the days ordained for me were written in your book
    before one of them came to be.
How precious to me are your thoughts, God!
    How vast is the sum of them!
Were I to count them,
    they would outnumber the grains of sand—
    when I awake, I am still with you.

1

Made by God

She chose to believe
and it set her free.

To discover who we've been made to be, we must start at the beginning. I believe the answers to our biggest questions about life and our purpose begin with one simple yet mysterious and profound truth: we have been made.

We must ask ourselves what we believe about the foundational questions of life. Why do we exist? What is the meaning of it all? The Greek philosopher Socrates said, "an unexamined life is not worth living."[1] It can be easy to take our existence for granted, to go about the motions and never look for the answers to some of life's greatest questions. One of the biggest questions we can ask is, "How did I get here?" Have you ever wondered how this expansive, sophisticated, beautiful world began?

Our belief about how and why we are here will determine the course of our entire lives and change the way we see ourselves. It will shape our sense of worth. It will determine our sense of purpose. What we believe as young girls—and eventually as women—about how we came to exist determines the way we understand ourselves, our lives, and our value. It is the substance upon which we build our identity.

Just as Socrates said the unexamined life isn't worth living, I wonder if the unexamined faith is worth believing? Maybe you've been raised in a Christian home. You fell asleep to stories of Noah's ark. You are familiar with the creation story and you believe in God, but have you used the mind He's given you to examine your beliefs? Or maybe all you've heard is that there was a "big bang" in the cosmos and billions of years later we are here due to evolution.

There are two primary viewpoints on how the universe and life as we know it began. The atheistic view is that life resulted outside of intelligent design or divine intervention. The theistic view is that life is the result of intelligent design, that life had a creator or a supernatural beginning.

If you believe you evolved over billions or millions of years and originated without any divine intervention, what does this say about the meaning of your life? Are you an accident? Should you really be here? What is the purpose for your life, and what happens when it's over?

If you believe the universe was divinely created, what does this mean? Could it be that, before the beginning of time, you were chosen to be here? Is there a unique purpose for your life? Is there something after it's over?

In our culture, there is a battle between science and religion, and many claim you can only side with one. Some physicists believe the universe burst into existence out of nothing. However, even atheists agree with theists—that the universe had a beginning.

In his book *The Case for a Creator*, Lee Strobel, an author and former legal editor who was once an atheist, interviewed Stephen C. Meyer, an author and former geophysicist. He quoted Meyer as saying, "If it's true there's a beginning to the universe, as modern cosmologists now agree, then this implies a cause that transcends the universe. If the laws of physics are fine-tuned to permit life, as contemporary physicists are discovering, then perhaps there's a designer who fine-tuned them. If there's information in the cell, as molecular biology shows, then this suggests intelligent design."[2]

Scientists of all worldviews agree that our universe is finely tuned, meaning there is a precision of physical laws and constants that must be exact for life to exist. If any of these constants, such as the gravitational force that holds the moon in its orbit or the strong force that holds the atoms together, changes by a tiny fraction of a percent, life becomes unsustainable. This convinces me that our world was intelligently designed with precision, order, and intention.

On his journey toward faith, Strobel realized,

To continue in atheism, I would need to believe that nothing produces everything, non-life produces life, randomness produces fine-tuning, chaos produces information, unconsciousness produces consciousness, and non-reason produces reason. I simply didn't have that much faith.[3]

It takes faith to believe in God. Like Strobel, I believe it takes even more faith to believe this all just happened.

There are many scientific theories about how the first living cell appeared and how life has evolved since. However, these theories don't speak to the origin of human consciousness, our emotions, or our innate search for meaning. Philanthropist John Templeton, despite not adhering to an orthodox theology, still posed a great question: "Would it not be strange if a universe without purpose accidentally created humans who are so obsessed with purpose?"[4] We are physical and spiritual beings. We are looking for spiritual answers our material world cannot provide.

The Bible tells the story of a wealthy man named Job. He was an upright man who did the right thing. Job went on to have every good thing taken from him and to experience immense sorrow and suffering. Job questions God and then God speaks to him and says,

> "Where were you when I laid the earth's foundation?
>> Tell me, if you understand.
> Who marked off its dimensions? Surely you know!
>> Who stretched a measuring line across it?
> On what were its footings set,
>> or who laid its cornerstone—
> while the morning stars sang together
>> and all the angels shouted for joy?" (Job 38:4–7)

Radiant sunsets, gnarled oak trees, a harvest moon, fireflies in summer, a child's giggle—the beauty around us speaks of a beautiful creator. No, it didn't all just happen:

For since the creation of the world God's invisible qualities—his eternal power and divine nature—have been clearly seen, being understood from what has been made, so that people are without excuse. (Romans 1:20)

God has revealed Himself through creation because of what has been made. Creation praises the Creator. God is the great artist, the master designer, the chief architect of all things wild, lovely, and beautiful. His evidence surrounds us, and because of this, we have no excuse not to believe in a higher purpose.

As a little girl, I never doubted the existence of a creator—I saw God's fingerprints all around me—in the giant trees hovering above our home upon the hill; in the glorious sunsets of pinks, purples, and oranges painted on the canvas of the evening sky; in the miracles of roly-poly bugs and shooting stars. Even as a little girl, my spirit knew the beauty around me was evidence for the God who made it all.

The universe is not looking out for you, but the One who breathed it into existence is.

The universe is not looking out for you, but the One who breathed it into existence is. As you embark on this journey to discover the life you've been made for, will you choose to believe that you've been made? This belief is the foundation on which you will build your understanding of who you are and who you've been created to be.

Be Still and Be Loved

A TIME TO REFLECT

How does what you believe about how you came to exist influence your sense of identity and purpose?

God,
I see Your fingerprints all around me in what You have created. I believe because of what has been made. Show me the path to life as I put my faith in You.

2

Made to Know God

She's discovering eternal truths that tell her who she is and of the One who holds all things together.

*I*t is one thing to believe in God, but it takes more faith to really know Him. The Bible is the bridge that takes us from believing in God to really understanding and knowing Him. The Bible is the best-selling book of all time, with an estimated five billion copies in print throughout the world.

Even as a little girl growing up in a somewhat religious home, I knew it was sacred. Dressed in my Sunday best, my little ears soaked in stories about Jesus as I attended church. The Bible held a prominent position on our bookshelf, though we never read it at home. Its fine print and old-fashioned words were intimidating. To me, the Bible was mysterious, overwhelming, and way over my head. It seemed so holy that it should be untouchable, so I kept my distance.

However, when my life fell apart due to severe depression at the age of eighteen, I was desperate for hope and began to read it for the first time. As I began to pore over the Psalms and Gospels, I went from believing in God to having a deeper knowledge and understanding of Him.

While it is considered one complete book, the Bible is a collection of many books written by many authors over a span of about 1,500 years. The books of the Bible were written by everyday people inspired by God to record wisdom and events. The Old Testament, which wrapped up its writings around 450 BC, records events before the birth of Christ and documents God's relationships with the Jewish people. The New Testament captures the life and ministry of Jesus and His followers during the first century and records the many miracles Jesus performed and the struggles faced by early Christians.

I was desperate for hope.

The Bible is unmatched by other published works for many reasons. For one, the Bible foretells detailed events years and even centuries before they happened. There are about 2,500 prophecies or passages in the Bible that reflect communication from God and tell of interpretations, warnings, or predictions. These prophecies are about everything from natural disasters to global politics, the future of the nation of Israel, the coming of a Messiah or Savior of the world, and the fate of humanity.

Through the prophet Isaiah, God says, "Remember the former things, those of long ago; I am God, and there is no other; I am God, and there is none like me. I make known the end from the beginning, from ancient times, what is still to come" (Isaiah 46:9–10). This speaks to God's eternal nature and His sovereignty. He is timeless—for He declares the end from the beginning.

I am most compelled by the numerous biblical prophecies Jesus has fulfilled. The Old Testament prophets recorded detailed signs about the coming of the Messiah, the Savior of the world. There are over three hundred Old Testament prophecies that Jesus fulfilled. As I consider this astounding fact, my faith is strengthened, as it is simply not plausible to attribute this to mere coincidence.

Out of all ancient documents, the Bible has the most surviving copies that can be examined for variants or errors. Many of Jesus' followers were severely persecuted, yet they didn't stop spreading His message. The records of the New Testament are consistent and accurate. Even though the Bible has many authors and was written over a long period of time, it has a consistent and coherent message of God's love and redemption.

Some of the doubts people have about the Bible arise because of the stories recorded in the Old Testament. The Red Sea parted, Jonah was swallowed by a large fish, a flood covered the earth, and the sun stood still. We might wrestle with these stories and question if they really happened. We may wonder if they are literal or if they are mere fables intended to emphasize God's almighty power. If God exists and is so powerful, and He created something beautiful out of nothing, then with Him the supernatural is possible. Because life itself is a miracle, the miraculous is possible.

The apostle Paul wrote, "All Scripture is God-breathed and is useful for teaching, rebuking, correcting and training in righteousness, so that the servant of God may be thoroughly equipped for every good work" (2 Timothy 3:16–17). I love the word picture that "God-breathed" paints in my mind. I envision God breathing words of truth and revelation through His Spirit to the many authors of the Bible who recorded them. Centuries later our eyes glide across the pages of this ancient text that has been like a lighthouse guiding billions of people throughout human history. As it has for centuries, its words are read every day in churches and homes, in hospital rooms, at weddings, and at funerals throughout the world.

I think of the strong women of our past who endured civil wars, world wars, famine, plagues, or other difficult times, and who turned to these God-breathed words for hope, comfort, and understanding. I consider how countless women today do the same. There are good works God has prepared in advance for you too. The Bible will equip you to live out these unique and good purposes guiding your steps every day.

Today, we are blessed to still have the Bible's ancient but eternal wisdom at our fingertips (and on our phones) to guide and strengthen us for the good things we have been called to do. As we read them, the Bible's words penetrate our hearts, giving us courage in our current circumstances. While we won't generally hear an audible voice from God, He has given you the gift of His Word because He wants to speak to you.

What are the questions you have for God? What circumstance in your life needs His eternal wisdom? Be willing to turn off the notifications and shut out the noise and make space in your life to hear from the One who made you and loves you.

Jesus says, "Man shall not live on bread alone, but on every word that comes from the mouth of God" (Matthew 4:4). Scripture is our soul food. It sustains and nourishes us for this life. It guides us through our darkest days and equips us for our best days. James 1:21 says the Word of God has the power to save our souls. What else in the world has the power to do that?

The Bible is God's way of revealing Himself to you. Through Scripture, God has bridged the gap that has separated us from a mere knowledge of Him to a heartfelt understanding of who He really is. You were not only made by God; you were made to know God. Augustine of Hippo said, "The Holy Scriptures are our letters from home."[1] These letters are designed to guide us through this sometimes brutal but beautiful life. Will you read this love letter and let it change your life?

Be Still and Be Loved

A TIME TO REFLECT

How can you allow the Bible's wisdom to transform your life?

God,
Thank You for Your love letter to me. Open my heart to receive Your truth. Let it nourish my soul and guide me all the days of my life.

3

Made for a Relationship with God

She found a redeeming love she'll never outrun.

While I had a deep faith in God as a little girl and felt His presence whenever I stared at the starry night sky or watched the sun set over the city beneath our hill, God often felt distant, mysterious, and even like a stranger. I believed in God as the creator, but I didn't comprehend that I could really know Him personally like a friend.

Each night before bed, my mom would come into my room and kneel next to me as I lay down in my bed hugging "Gund," my stuffed dinosaur. My mom still smelled of the perfume she wore to work, and I looked forward to our evening prayers and her soft kisses. Together we would pray:

Now I lay me down to sleep,
I pray the Lord my soul to keep.
If I should die before I wake,
I pray the Lord my soul to take.

Then I would close by saying, "God bless Mommy and Daddy and Timmy and Sunny (our golden retriever) and Grandma and Nana and everyone in the whole world . . . except the bad guys." The prayers my parents guided me through before dinner and bedtime taught me I could talk to God, but I wasn't convinced He heard me or that my prayers mattered.

Years later, when I picked up that Bible in the hospital, I discovered that not only was I made by God, but that I was created to know God through a personal relationship with Jesus, His Son. As I pored over the Gospels of Matthew, Mark, Luke, and John (the first four books of the New Testament), I discovered that Jesus loves the broken and came to offer them hope and healing. I went from believing in God as creator to recognizing my need for a Savior and finding one in Jesus.

God, who is all-powerful and the creator of all things, made a way to bridge the separation between Himself and humankind. He entered our story and lived and loved among us as fully God and fully man through the person of Jesus Christ. By taking on flesh and bone, walking among us two thousand years ago, and dying and rising from the dead, God revealed His true character and divinity through the life and teachings of Jesus.

John 3:16 says, "For God so loved the world that he gave his one and only Son, that whoever believes in him shall not perish but have eternal life." God came down to rescue and redeem us through His Son Jesus because of His boundless love and desire for eternal relationship with us. No other "god" has done this, defeating death in the process.

The case for the life and resurrection of Jesus is compelling and cannot be ignored. There are over five hundred Greek manuscripts of the New Testament in existence. Even historians outside the Bible, like Josephus, have documented the life of Jesus. There is little dispute among ancient historians that Jesus died from crucifixion. After Jesus died, His disciples were terrified they would be crucified as well, but shortly after Jesus' resurrection these same disciples began boldly proclaiming that Jesus was who He claimed to be. They continued to spread His message, enduring persecution to their death.

Following the resurrection, even the enemies of Jesus admitted His tomb was empty. First Corinthians 15:6 states that Jesus appeared to over five hundred people after He died. He appeared to skeptics and believers, men and women.

The great Christian apologist C. S. Lewis reflected on the unique divinity of Christ:

A man who was merely a man and said the sort of things Jesus said would not be a great moral teacher. . . . You must make your choice. Either this man was, and is, the Son of God: or else a madman or something worse. You can shut Him up for a fool, you can spit at Him and kill Him as a demon; or you can fall at His feet and call Him Lord and God. *But let us not come with any patronising nonsense about His being a great human teacher. He has not left that open to us.*[1]

Preacher John Duncan came to a similar conclusion, saying, "Christ either deceived mankind by conscious fraud, or he was himself deluded and self-deceived, or he was Divine. There is no getting out of this trilemma. It is inexorable."[2] At one point, every person must decide whether they believe Jesus was a liar or lunatic or Lord.

As the ultimate hope for our souls, Jesus offers us a new way to live. Are you tired from striving and from feelings of unworthiness? Jesus said, "Come to me, all you who are weary and burdened, and I will give you rest. Take my yoke upon you and learn from me, for I am gentle and humble in heart, and you will find rest for your souls. For my yoke is easy and my burden is light" (Matthew 11:28–30).

While my breakdown was difficult, it exposed my self-focused and shallow way of living and led me to experience the healing power of Jesus in a way that changed me forever.

> **"There has never been a moment in your life when you haven't been loved by Jesus."**

Perhaps the most compelling thing about Jesus is the way He transforms lives. One of my best friends, Christie, has bravely shared her testimony. Midway through high school after a series of heartaches she became addicted to cocaine, and by the age of eighteen had had two abortions. "I was really broken at that point," Christie said. "I had lost a huge sense of who I was." A friend invited Christie to an early morning prayer service. "God spoke so clearly to me that morning through the pastor. He said, 'There has never been a moment in your life when you haven't been loved by the Lord.' I thought back to all those bad times in my life—when I was in the recovery room of Planned Parenthood, when I was doing cocaine, when I was sleeping with that boy, when I was mocking God at a party. Yet even during all those moments, Jesus still loved me."

Let that sink in. There has never been a moment in your life when you haven't been loved by Jesus. Romans 8:38–39 affirms this: "For I am convinced that neither death nor life, neither angels nor demons, neither the present nor the future, nor any powers, neither height nor depth, nor anything else in all creation, will be able to separate us from the love of God that is in Christ Jesus our Lord." Our unbelief cannot. Our bad decisions cannot. Our pride and self-sufficiency cannot separate us from the love of Christ. You are never too far gone from God, and, in this life, you will never escape His love for you.

Not only are we offered a love we can't outrun, but we are given an identity that can't be shaken. Author and priest Brennan Manning wrote, "Our identity rests in God's relentless tenderness for us revealed in Jesus Christ."[3] Manning also encouraged a definition of self that is especially countercultural today: "Define yourself radically as one beloved by God. This is the true self. Every other identity is illusion."[4]

When Jesus was crucified, our sin or anything that separates us from the holiness of God was also put to death. When Jesus defeated the grave and rose again on the third day, our sins were forgiven, and the gift of salvation was given to us who believe. The path to eternal life is simple. Romans 10:9 says, "If you declare with your mouth, 'Jesus is Lord,' and believe in your heart that God raised him from the dead, you will be saved."

When we believe, we are given a new beginning. Second Corinthians 5:17 says, "Therefore, if anyone is in Christ, the new creation has come: The old has gone, the new is here!" Not only are we given new life, we are given a new identity. In Christ, we discover who we really are: radically loved without condition, completely forgiven, made to live forever, and never too far gone. We are invited to live life as His beloved and when we accept the invitation, everything changes. Are you ready to discover your true purpose and identity and live loved by God?

Be Still and Be Loved

A TIME TO REFLECT

How does what you believe about Jesus influence your life?

Jesus,
Thank You for the gift of forgiveness and eternal life. Help me define myself as radically loved by You as I seek You with all my heart. Take my life and make me who You created me to be.

4

Made in the Image of God

She's clothed in heaven's wonder.

I have vivid memories of sitting in art class as a shy school girl dressed in my green plaid jumper and white collared shirt. At the start of class, our art teacher held up the day's project: a piece of paper with a mosaic fruit bowl pieced together with bits of magazine clippings strategically placed side by side to resemble bananas, apples, and oranges. Next, she passed out stacks of old *National Geographic* magazines, construction paper, scissors, and glue and told us to get to work. Our final creations somewhat resembled her beautiful mosaic fruit bowl, each with their unique flair. Some kids' creations were made of teeny tiny pieces of magazine clippings, while others were made of chunky clippings. In some, bananas or oranges appeared to be falling out of the bowl while others stayed nicely put.

Similar to the way our creations resembled our teacher's artwork, human beings have been made to resemble or mirror God. Genesis 1:27 says, "So God created mankind in his own image, in the image of God he created them; male and female he created them." We have been made to bear the image of God through our miraculous existence. To bear an image of something is to resemble it or have likeness to it. Individually we would present an incomplete resemblance of God, but collectively as men, women, and children with different personalities, skin tones, and ethnicities, we mirror our Creator while at the same time falling short.

> **We have been made to bear the image of God through our miraculous existence.**

In the same way you are like your biological parents but are also different, you bear likeness to God. We are made to mirror God and to make His invisible attributes visible to this world for His glory, not our own. Pioneering physician Paul Brand and author Phillip Yancey wrote:

> Like a growing child absorbing traits from his parents, like a student learning from his professor, we can take on God's qualities—compassion, mercy, love, gentleness—and express them to a needy, broken world. As spirit, God remains invisible, relying on us to make that spirit visible.[1]

Jesus made that spirit visible when He became flesh. Can you think of a higher calling than to make the spirit and goodness of God visible through *your* life? This is the call that comes with being an image bearer of God.

Of all that has been created, humans have a unique dignity. We are unlike everything else in creation. Psalm 8 speaks beautifully to our inherent worth. The psalmist writes:

> When I consider your heavens,
> the work of your fingers,
> the moon and the stars,
> which you have set in place,
> what is mankind that you are mindful of them,
> human beings that you care for them?
>
> You have made them a little lower than the angels
> and crowned them with glory and honor.
> You made them rulers over the works of your hands;
> you put everything under their feet.
> (Psalm 8:3–6)

As women, we easily gloss over our divine dignity, taking it for granted or forgetting it altogether. We rarely, if ever, marvel at the way our heart beats on its own or how our fingerprint is different from billions of other fingerprints. Sometimes, shame overshadows our inherent sense of worth, and we seem to lose sight of the One who made us and gives us our significance. On the other hand, we can sometimes think a little too highly of ourselves, forgetting that apart from our Creator, we are nothing.

It took me some time to understand what it meant to be made in the image of God because I was so consumed by my own self-image. For much of my teen years and early twenties, I chased an ideal of the girl I thought I should be. In high school, on my full-length bedroom mirror were magazine clippings of runway and fitness models and celebrities who had my dream body and look. By daily admiring these photoshopped images, I overlooked the divine beauty within me and idolized other women who were fashioned by the same hands that fashioned me.

In the book of Romans, the apostle Paul talks about the foolishness of worshiping people and forgetting the Creator, a message that is so relevant to our culture today. He says, "For although they knew God, they neither glorified him as God nor gave thanks to him, but their thinking became futile and their foolish hearts were darkened. Although they claimed to be wise, they became fools and exchanged the glory of the immortal God for images made to look like a mortal human being and birds and animals and reptiles" (Romans 1:21–23).

We see the same principle in our culture today. Instead of looking to God in whose image we are divinely created, we can easily worship celebrities and influencers or even our friends. We might scroll through staged and filtered photos and compare ourselves to the women in them as we forget the God who made us all. In idolizing others we can worship the creation rather than the Creator who gave us all breath and made us equally valuable.

The ideal image we chase or hold of ourselves and others is an illusion. The pursuit of our ideal selves can prevent us from being a fully alive image bearer of God. The idol of self prevents us from bearing God's image to the world.

When we turn our gaze away from the One whose image we were fashioned in, and pursue the image of our ideal selves, we are falling for a cheapened life. Chasing the ever-elusive version of who you think you should be and what you should look like based on the world's ideals will leave you empty and insecure. But if you want to live a full and wholehearted life, give thanks to the God who breathed you into existence and made you beautifully in His image. Above all, seek to know God through Jesus by spending time with Him through reading the Bible, worship, prayer, and Christian community. As you do this, your life will begin to bear the invisible Spirit of God to your sphere of influence.

When we believe we have been handcrafted by the Creator of all that is good, our spirit is set at ease. Instead of sculpting ourselves to fit our own ideal, we look to the One whose image we bear for our true purpose and worth. We cease striving. We accept our divine spark and it shows as we make the people around us feel loved and known. We shine outward bringing light to the dark places. We accept our high calling to bear the image of a loving, compassionate God to a world that has lost its way. The world is waiting and hungry for you to make the beauty and goodness of God visible and to shine His radiant light in the unique way only you can.

Be Still and Be Loved

A TIME TO REFLECT

What does it look like to be an image bearer of God to a world desperate for love and truth?

God,
Thank You for the high and worthy calling
You have placed on my life as Your child.
Equip me to live loved by You and to bear
Your image to a world in desperate need of
Your love and truth.

5

Made with Love and Wonder

Made in the secret place, she's a masterpiece.

*D*id you know that according to scientists the odds of you being born are one in about four hundred trillion or *more*? The definition of a miracle is that an event is so unlikely it is pretty much impossible. By that definition, you are a miracle!

Have you considered how your toes wiggle, how your heart beats on its own, and how you have two eyes that allow you to see and take in the beauty of the world? Have you ever really considered the amazing truth that no one exactly like you has ever existed before in all of history?

In Psalm 139, the author David reflects on the way God has designed him and knows him. He says:

> For you created my inmost being;
>   you knit me together in my mother's womb.
> I praise you because I am fearfully and wonderfully made;
>   your works are wonderful,
>   I know that full well. (Psalm 139:13–14)

With praise on his lips, David acknowledges that it is God who gave him life and fashioned him within his mother's womb. Then he praises God for fearfully and wonderfully making him. The word "fearfully" is an easy word to get hung up on. It's not exactly a pleasant-sounding adjective that we would use to describe our friends or loved ones, but there is a proper and profound meaning for the word. The Old Testament Scriptures were originally written in Hebrew and were translated into many other languages.

The word "fearfully" comes from the Hebrew word *yare*, which translates "to stand in awe of," or "be awed." The root word also means reverence, honor, and respect.[1] To be fearfully made means to be made with awe, respect, reverence, and love. The word "wonderfully" comes from the Hebrew word *pala* meaning "inspiring delight, pleasure, or admiration; extremely good; marvelous."[2] You have been made with love and wonder.

To be fearfully and wonderfully made means knowing God created you with intention, purpose, wonder, beauty, and awe. David recognizes the miracle of his existence and thanks God in confidence for it. He knows full well God made something good when He made him.

I have seen a disturbing trend among girls and women—a trend I've partaken in. We see and affirm the beauty and wonder all around us: in our friends, in creation, and in filtered images on screens. However, we rarely recognize beauty in ourselves. In high school, as my friends and I were getting ready to go to dances or parties, we would take turns belittling our facial features or body parts in the mirror, trying to outdo one another with attacks on ourselves. It was as if self-disdain was a trophy we were trying to win and the girl who tore herself down the most, won. I reflect on those years and I imagine God looking down on His beloved masterpieces, saddened and heartbroken that His daughters would call themselves ugly, fat, unworthy, and unlovable.

To be fearfully and wonderfully made means knowing God created you with intention, purpose, wonder, beauty, and awe.

In verse 16 of Psalm 139, David says, "Your eyes saw my unformed body." God designed our bodies intentionally and calls them good. When's the last time you have called your body good? We are a generation of women and girls who are fixated on our bodies. Too many of us believe our worth is determined by what we weigh rather than who we are.

Our bodies are not projects that need fixing. They are phenomenally created instruments that allow us to live and love others. As believers, our bodies are the temples of the Holy Spirit (1 Corinthians 6:19).

Several years ago, I bought a 1961 vintage trailer I named Pearl. Her tires were road-ready and her axle was strong. She was equipped for camping trips up the coast to see California's rugged coastline and the giant redwood forests. She was prepared to hit the highway and take me on awesome adventures. But, instead of traveling, I spent those hours trying to make Pearl look perfect.

In the same way, I spent many years treating my body as if it were a project to be perfected. As I reflect on my younger years as a teen and a woman in my early twenties, I am saddened by the way I focused on how my body looked or didn't look. I now see how much fuller my life would have been if I could have fully appreciated the wonder of my body and embraced the life it enabled me to have.

It is estimated that in the US alone, twenty million women will suffer from a clinical eating disorder such as anorexia, bulimia, or EDNOS (eating disorder not otherwise specified) at some time in their life.[3] In high school, I took diet pills and struggled with disordered eating, occasionally bingeing and purging. I was fixated on trying to make my body look a way it wasn't designed to. Eating disorders are quick to rush in when an existential vacuum or void exists in a person's life. As one young woman shared with me years ago, "I was experiencing a major spiritual void in my life during the height of my eating disorder. I didn't know what my purpose was, and my eating disorder was a way for something to creep in and give me purpose."

One day, if we're given many years on this earth, we will be covered with wrinkles from head to toe. For those of us who spent our lives in constant body angst, we will finally realize our legacy is not measured by the size we wear, but by the life we have led. We'll come face to face with the truth that we are not only our body. We are a soul in a body that is temporal and deteriorating until it is one day healed and restored in heaven.

I had the privilege of interviewing a nine-year-old girl who knows full well that she has been fearfully and wonderfully made. Grace Anna Rodgers was born with a rare form of dwarfism called Conradi Hünermann syndrome. Doctors tried to get her mother Angela to abort her five different times. At three years old, Grace Anna's rendition of "The Star-Spangled Banner" went viral. Since then, millions have become endeared to her sweet spirit and happy personality, which she demonstrates through her speaking and singing. Soon thereafter she made an appearance on the *Today Show*. Grace Anna continues to light up the world around her through her contagious laugh and beautiful singing.

When I asked Angela about what it means to her that her daughter has been fearfully and wonderfully made, she said, "I think so many times in our society we focus only on what somebody looks like on the outside. To me, God has given each of us a specific way to represent Him. We have a specific purpose for how we look and for how we function. I think when God made Grace Anna in my belly, He knew how many people she was going to touch. He knew how she would change lives." Angela added, "When we get to the point where we realize it's not about us, it's about Him, our view starts to change dramatically."[4]

Being wonderfully made is about praising God for the miracle of your existence and thanking Him that you are alive. It's about knowing "full well" that God's works are wonderful, including you, and refusing to say or believe otherwise. When you have a high and holy view of God, you have a healthy view of yourself. Being fearfully and wonderfully made is about rising above your insecurities and agreeing in faith that when God created you, He created something beautiful, someone awe-inspiring, and someone to be respected. It's about silencing the lies in your head that tell you you're not enough and praising

God for the unique way He has created you. When we believe that we have been made with such love, intention, and respect, our natural response is to stand tall in security and to worship and praise God for the life He has given us.

Let's be women who praise God for the marvelous way He made us, even the parts that seem imperfect or broken. Most of all, let's be women who praise God for who He is. As I close out this chapter, I challenge you to memorize Psalm 139:14: "I praise you because I am fearfully and wonderfully made; your works are wonderful, I know that full well." I encourage you to speak these true words over yourself. With time, it is possible for you to come to believe and accept that you truly are wonderfully made. This truth can change your entire life.

Be Still and Be Loved

A TIME TO REFLECT

How can you praise God with your life and take Him at His word when He says you have been wonderfully made?

God,
Thank You for creating me in love and wonder.
I praise You because I have been lovingly and
wonderfully created in Your image. Help me
rest in the truth that You have made me beau-
tifully to praise You with my life.

6

Made to Glorify God

She gladly gives God the spotlight.

We live in a self-glorifying culture. The path to happiness seems paved with self-worship and self-promotion. We see celebrities, professional athletes, and influencers get rewarded for their self-exaltation. They get the golden ticket and the rest of us try to follow suit or wonder why we're not quite enough. Their way of living sparkles and shines, but eventually the glitter wears off. The "likes" stop coming. Someone else shinier comes along. Their fans or followers turn their backs on them. We have bought into the lie that ultimate happiness is found when we self-actualize, which means "to realize fully one's potential."[1]

As a teen, I lived in constant self-focus. I prided myself on how I looked or performed in school and athletic activities. If I got attention from a guy, got an A on my exam, or scored a goal in soccer, I was proud of myself. I felt like I was worthy and had significance. But if I fell short of my self-imposed expectations, I was deflated. I'm grateful that in coming undone, I realized how empty it was to live for myself when it was God who gave me breath and every good thing. Finding myself as broken as a girl could be in the hospital was one of the best things that happened to me because it emptied me of everything I had built my worth and identity on. It freed me from myself and led me to know Jesus intimately and personally in a way that has transformed my life for the best.

Our true purpose is popularly summarized in the Westminster Shorter Catechism, which says our chief end or purpose is "to glorify God, and to enjoy him for ever."[2] In the Old Testament, the word "glory" means splendor or greatness. In the New Testament it means "dignity, honor, praise and worship."[3] To glorify God means to recognize God's greatness and to worship Him and give Him praise. Author and pastor John Piper says, "'Glorifying' means feeling and thinking and acting in ways that reflect his greatness, that make much of God, that give evidence of the supreme greatness of all his attributes and the all-satisfying beauty of his manifold perfections."[4] Piper has also said, "God is most glorified in us when we are most satisfied in Him."[5] Don't you want to be a woman who makes much of God, whose life gives evidence for His goodness and beauty?

As God's image bearers, our chief purpose is to glorify Him with our lives, to enjoy His goodness, and to make Him known. God does not need us to glorify Him. We can't add to or take away His glory, but as followers of Christ, we can honor, praise, and worship Him through our thoughts, actions, and relationships. When we live in a way that genuinely glorifies God, we are the most alive and happy. If we miss out on this chief purpose of our lives, we miss out on living our best lives.

The author of the book of Acts wrote, "For in him we live and move and have our being" (Acts 17:28). Every breath we take is because God has allowed it. We are dust apart from Him. It is one thing to have confidence in our self and our abilities, but it is another to become prideful of them. Glorifying God requires a posture of humility. When we live a life fixed on adoring and praising God, our eyes turn away from ourselves, and we actually become more emotionally healthy in the process. We are happier when we are living for God rather than striving to make ourselves worthy of love and attention. We are also more enjoyable to be around because our gaze shifts from inward to outward.

> **When we live in a way that genuinely glorifies God, we are the most alive and happy.**

First Corinthians 10:31 says, "So whether you eat or drink or whatever you do, do it all for the glory of God." What would it look like for you to glorify God in all you do? Part of this looks like acknowledging that the gifts, talents, abilities, and blessings you have flow from God and are not of your own making. The other part is joyfully experiencing these things as good gifts from God.

It can be easier to glorify God when things are going well, but we can also do so during seasons of disappointment and suffering. Over the last several years, through a young women's conference I help direct, I've had the privilege of getting to know a phenomenal woman who has glorified God through the good and hard days of her life. At the age of thirteen, Bethany Hamilton lost her left arm when she was attacked by a fourteen-foot tiger shark while surfing. Prior to the attack, Bethany was on course to become one of the world's top female surfers.

Just one month after losing her arm, Bethany got back on her board and within two years had won her first national surfing title, becoming a worldwide inspiration. The world has since watched in awe as she has pushed the limits, dominated the water, and charged some of the world's biggest waves. Through it all, she has remained humble and has given God glory during the good and hard times.

When deciding whether or not to do interviews following the attack, she told her mom, "I'm okay with doing interviews if you guys think that God can use me."[6] Though she'd rather be surfing than be in a TV interview or on a stage, Bethany has come to accept the platform God has given her and used it to point others to Jesus. She shared in her book *Soul Surfer: A True Story of Faith, Family, and Fighting to Get Back on the Board*: "I don't really want people looking to me for inspiration. I just want to be a sign along the way that points toward heaven."[7]

In our culture, it seems like the girl who elevates herself gets the most attention. The girl with the most followers gets the guy, gets the book deal, and gets her dreams realized. But there is another way to live. We can live in a way that shines the spotlight on God, knowing that He is the giver of every good and perfect gift (James 1:17).

I have come to believe that any good in me is God in me. As I enjoy God and the physical and spiritual gifts He has placed in my life, I naturally glorify Him and experience great joy and happiness in the process. When I look back on my teenage years, which I spent detached from God, I see the bottomless void I was trying to fill by trying to make myself captivating and worthy of attention. When we turn away from our self-centered pursuits and accept that our chief purpose is to adore and enjoy God, we really begin to shine. The heaviness in our hearts slowly begins to lighten as we take the pressure off ourselves to find our purpose and relax into the destiny God has for us: to be loved by Christ, to love others well, and to make Him known.

Be Still and Be Loved

A TIME TO REFLECT

How can you glorify God through the gifts and passions He's given you?

God,
Thank You for inviting me into a greater story—to live fully alive satisfied in You. I acknowledge that every good and perfect gift in my life comes from You and I resolve to glorify You in all I do and say so that others may know of Your goodness and love.

7

Made to Bloom

Even in the dry and stormy seasons, she is still blooming.

My husband and I recently bought our first grown-up house with a yard. A yard with weeds. To inspire me in my new job of gardening, I purchased a pair of baby blue and pink Crocs (so fashionable, I know!) to accompany a monstrous-sized straw hat. We all know a girl needs the right getup for the job. I quickly realized that 75 percent of my job as a reluctant gardener was weeding and pruning so that my plants and flowers could thrive. It was clear to see that if I didn't pull those weeds up by their deep roots, they would quickly overtake my Douglas iris, desert mallow, and lily of the Nile blooms that thrive in our coastal Santa Barbara climate. And if I didn't prune back dead and struggling branches, my plants would wither.

Each time I put on my dorky gardening outfit and gloves, unplug from my devices, and am left alone with my thoughts to work in our little yard, I find my mind ruminating on the countless spiritual principles gardening offers. Just as these sinister weeds were choking out the life from my precious flowers, the weeds in my own life were suffocating good things and keeping me from truly blooming. I considered the weeds of envy, comparison, distraction, unbelief, fear, and over-indulgence that were keeping me from the life I was made for.

We are made to pull our own weeds and tend to our own garden. One way to invite God to transform your life is to cut out the things that are robbing you of peace and joy. In my case, one weed was alcohol. I grew up with stories from my mom about her life growing up. Her father, my grandfather, would abuse amphetamines during the day and alcohol at night. This led to frequent drinking, rage, and fights, some of which led to calls to the police. My mom is the most resilient person I know, and she chose a better path. Still, I knew alcoholism ran deep in my family's roots.

On my high school graduation day, dozens of close friends and relatives gathered in my family's home to celebrate the close of a chapter and the dawning of a new one. I was surrounded by people who cared about me, but all I wanted was to disappear. Anxiety enveloped me, panic crept in. I ran upstairs to my brother's closet where I had hidden a beer left over from a friend's party. I chugged as much as I could as quickly as I could, hoping it would make me loosen up. That was when I let alcohol into my life.

Three years later I went to Las Vegas to celebrate my twenty-first birthday. Once again, I was battling severe depression and even suicidal thoughts. To celebrate my first legal drink, my friend ordered me a glass of red wine. With my index finger, I skimmed the circumference of the wine glass, inhaling the rich aroma. It was in that moment I felt God call me to give up drinking. I made a commitment in that Vegas casino that for the sake of my mental health I would no longer have alcohol be a part of my life. I would live sober.

Pulling the weed of alcohol out of my life was an unpopular, but very personal, decision that has protected my well-being. I realized that with my mental health struggles, keeping alcohol a part of my life would intensify my depression and put me at risk for alcoholism. I decided I didn't want anything in my life that was going to prevent me from thriving.

Even as we pull the weeds from our life, we must remain rooted to God and trust Him to be our source of life that allows us to thrive and bloom. Jesus says, "I am the true vine, and my Father is the gardener. He cuts off every branch in me that bears no fruit, while every branch that does bear fruit he prunes so that it will be even more fruitful" (John 15:1–2). Jesus continues, "Remain in me, as I also remain in you. No branch can bear fruit by itself; it must remain in the vine. Neither can you bear fruit unless you remain in me" (John 15:4).

Choose to live in God and make your home in Him. Trust Him as your master gardener. As you do, His loving Spirit will cut away the dead pieces of your life and prune the parts that need to be more fruitful. Then, as you remain in Christ, you will thrive and bloom even more.

Gardening also has a lot to teach us about the seasons. We know from our lives there are seasons of pain and sorrow and seasons of abundance and growth. There will be seasons in our lives when we are thriving and others when we are barely surviving.

But we know that every season has an end, followed by a season with a new beginning. God has given you everything you need to bloom right where you are whatever season you are in.

The Bible tells us we have "every spiritual blessing in Christ" (Ephesians 1:3). You are digging unseen roots in dry, hard places, and God will equip you to survive the desert and winter seasons of your life. He will be your strength. You must only remain in Him and take it breath by breath. The Bible says, "Though the fig tree does not bud and there are no grapes on the vines, though the olive crop fails and the fields produce no food . . . yet I will rejoice in the LORD, I will be joyful in God my Savior" (Habakkuk 3:17–18). Resolve to worship God even in the barren seasons when it seems like you will never bloom again. God is doing an unseen work deep in your soul, and only He knows what beautiful seasons and good gifts lie ahead.

I never used to see value in the dry or stormy seasons of my life. To be honest, I often need to be on the other side of my struggles before I see the value. I usually fight against my hard seasons with all my might, desperate for an escape and eager to see an end. But the more difficult times I have endured, the more I see that my trials have always been periods of invisible growth. In those hard seasons, I dig deep roots beneath the surface in secret places that will one day help me flourish. My mental health battles have cultivated resilience. My pain has been transformed into purpose. Good fruit can come from hard places. Going through a breakup, enduring a health crisis, or experiencing a broken dream, while very difficult, can shape you and one day make you bloom even more beautifully.

For her royal wedding, Kate Middleton chose to include the flower lily-of-the-valley in her bouquet. The delicate looking blooms don't appear tough enough to survive the extremes of the coldest winters, but they can shrug off bone chilling temperatures. The flower prefers very cold weather, which results in more beautiful blossoms in the spring. The harsher the winter, the more beautifully it blooms.

Some of the loveliest women I've met are women who have endured harsh seasons, but by inviting Jesus into the painful parts of their journey, they have emerged strong and beautiful. Instead of growing bitter or hard-hearted, they allow God to cultivate the fruit of the Spirit in their lives: "love, joy, peace, patience, kindness, goodness, faithfulness, gentleness, and self-control" (Galatians 5:22–23 NLT). As they bloom they invite others to see the goodness of a God who is always faithful through every season of their lives.

If you're barely surviving a season you'd rather not be in, hide yourself in the shadow of the Almighty and find refuge in His presence. Be still and ask God to fight for you—to dig deep roots in your life so one day you can bloom again.

Be Still and Be Loved

A TIME TO REFLECT

What weeds are God calling you to pull from your life, and how can you bloom and flourish right where God has you in this season?

Lord,
Thank You for the garden that is my life. You are my master gardener. Help me remain in You and give me strength and wisdom as I pull the weeds that are keeping me from truly blooming. Help me trust that even in the hard, stormy seasons of my life, You are at work for my good. Help me bloom and bear fruit for Your glory.

8

Made for Beauty

Her beauty lies not in what is seen, but in what is unseen.

Creation shouts out the glory of God through all that is wild and free. Trek the steep crevices of the Sierras in winter, explore the Great Barrier Reef, meander through your favorite park, or go for a walk on an endless stretch of coastline—beauty invites us to live in wonder and awe.

We come alive in beauty's presence and our souls find rest. The psalmist prayed, "One thing I ask from the LORD, this only do I seek: that I may dwell in the house of the LORD all the days of my life, to gaze on the beauty of the LORD" (Psalm 27:4). The beauty of God draws us closer to Him in worship.

To unearth the purpose of beauty, we must revisit the creation story. From the moment God first spoke—and light engulfed the darkness—an eternal masterpiece began unfolding. He created day and night, the sky, sea, and land. He made the sun and moon. He filled the sea with living creatures and covered the sky with birds. He created animals large and small to roam the earth.

Then something extraordinary took place. God formed a man in His image from the dust of the earth (Genesis 2:7). With each act of creation, God was pleased. Each work of creation became more intricate than the last. And then the pinnacle of creation was formed: God breathed life into Eve and woman was fashioned. Eve was the crowning beauty of creation, wonderfully made to bear the image of God in a unique way.

As John and Stasi Eldredge write in *Captivating: Unveiling the Mystery of a Woman's Soul:*

> Woman is the crown of creation—the most intricate, dazzling creature on earth. She has a crucial role to play, a destiny of her own.
>
> And she too, bears the image of God (Gen. 1:26), but in a way that only the feminine can speak. What can we learn from her? God wanted to reveal something about himself, so he gave us Eve. When you are with a woman, ask yourself, "What is she telling me about God?"[1]

How does it feel to be one of God's most exquisite and intricately designed creations? Do you accept the inherent worth He's created in you? You have a matchless role to play in the adventure He's mapped out just for you.

Men and women are typically very different from one another.

My husband Paul is always looking for the next dangerous adventure and is happy living with just the bare necessities. When we met, he was living in what we affectionately called "the hole." His metal bunkbed was made before he was born and on his sink was a single toothbrush. His patio overflowed with surfboards, a kayak, an entire fleet of bikes, a skateboard, and a barbeque.

I saw past his poor decorating skills, and we said "I do" three years after we met. We are one year into what we hope will be our forever home, and I can't stop filling it with textured pillows, scented candles, flowers, framed photographs, and timeless pieces of furniture. I'm obsessively scouring the internet for my next purchase, endlessly on a hunt for something to make our space even more lovely. As women, we've been created to inhale and exhale beauty.

One of my side-hustles is portrait photography. I especially love photographing girls and women. I have yet to photograph one guy who will twirl for me. I love when a girl or a woman gasps and flashes a radiant smile after I show her a sneak peek of herself on my camera. When we believe we are beautiful for who God made us to be, we can live at rest and pour into others, knowing we are enough because we are God's and He calls us good.

For many years, I chased an unrealistic and worldly standard of beauty—sometimes going to modeling agencies for casting calls only to hear them tell me I needed to lose fifteen pounds. After these rejections, my dieting and bingeing intensified. I thought that if I could just grace the pages of magazines, it would mean that I had arrived and that beauty, success, and prosperity were mine for the rest of my life. Like my younger self, too many girls and women are building their lives on how they look.

Building our life on our outward appearance is like building a hillside mansion on shifting sand. Physical beauty cannot sustain the weight of our true worth. We know that physical beauty fades:

> Your beauty should not come from outward adornment, such as elaborate hairstyles and the wearing of gold jewelry or fine clothes. Rather, it should be that of your inner self, the unfading beauty of a gentle and quiet spirit, which is of great worth in God's sight. For this is the way the holy women of the past who put their hope in God used to adorn themselves. (1 Peter 3:3–5)

When I am getting ready to go on a date night or attend a social gathering, I thoughtfully pick out my outfit and adorn myself with light makeup and turquoise jewelry. One night, as I looked in the mirror, I imagined how I would act around our friends and wondered if they would find me absolutely captivating. And then something funny happened. I sensed God inviting me to step away from my reflection, and these words flooded my mind: *It's not about how you look; it's about how you make others feel.*

True beauty is not in what is seen, but what is unseen.

Now as I get ready, I repeat these words to myself as a reminder that my true beauty is not in what is seen, but in what is unseen. It is in what is felt and experienced. As much as I enjoy looking nice, I want my beauty to come from my inner self—from who I am. I want to have an unfading beauty that invites others to believe that God is good and loves them more than they can imagine. I want to laugh out loud, but I want a quiet spirit—a spirit that is at rest because I know in Christ I am whole and free. I want to be like those holy women of the past—wise, steadfast, strong, and kind, with a beauty of great worth in God's sight.

God made you for beauty because He wants to use you to display His goodness and character to the world. And He made you to delight in beauty because He wants you to delight in Him, the author of all things beautiful. What would it look like to stop chasing society's standard of beauty and cultivate a heart at rest? When people are with you, what is your presence telling them about God? You have an authentic beauty to unveil. The world is waiting.

Be Still and Be Loved

A TIME TO REFLECT

What would it look like to cultivate a beauty that never fades?

God,
Thank You for the majesty of creation that draws me near to You. Help me let go of unrealistic standards of beauty that keep me imprisoned and self-focused. Cultivate in me an inner beauty that comes from having a spirit that is at rest. Make me a willing vessel that unveils Your beauty to a world desperate for hope.

9

Made for Something More

She is discovering there are far greater things ahead than all she is leaving behind.

Do you ever feel like you've been made for more than the life you're living? Eternity is set in our hearts and heaven is where we're ultimately made for. Without even knowing it, our heart longs for the healing, perfection, and redemption that awaits us in heaven. In the meantime, we exist in this beautiful but broken world and are made to find meaning and purpose in it.

Having worked closely with countless girls and young women over the years, I am saddened by nothing more than seeing even one missing out on the life of purpose and joy that God has for her. I'm heartbroken when the allure of the world outshines the Spirit-filled path that leads to life and true joy. As someone who has chased what the world offers, I know how captivating a life of self-sufficiency, freedom, pleasure, influence, status, and ease can be. I also know it leads to emptiness and devastation. Jesus warns us, "Enter through the narrow gate. For wide is the gate and broad is the road that leads to destruction, and many enter through it. But small is the gate and narrow the road that leads to life, and only a few find it" (Matthew 7:13–14).

I have seen the ways of the world break too many women. I don't want it to break you. Living a life of pleasure contrary to God's ways eventually results in a broken person with a broken life. The wide road leads to a life of unnecessary damage—drug and alcohol addiction, abortion, STDs, broken hearts, debt, relationship drama, and poor mental health, to name a few. On the other hand, doing life God's way, while not free from suffering, leads to an abundant life. "The precepts of the LORD are right, giving joy to the heart. The commands of the LORD are radiant, giving light to the eyes" (Psalm 19:8). Don't you want that for your own life? Don't you want to be a woman who is fully alive and radiant with a beautiful light in her eyes? A precept is a guiding principle or rule that, when obeyed, regulates our behavior and conduct. God's precepts are designed to give us a life of more—more peace, joy, freedom, and purpose.

There's a widely circulated meme of a little girl clinging to a tattered little teddy bear. In the illustration, Jesus is kneeling before the girl with one arm outstretched before her, asking for her teddy bear. "But I love it," she says. "Just trust Me," Jesus tells the little girl. Behind Jesus' back is a giant new teddy bear He wants to give her in exchange for the one she's holding on to.

Like this little girl, we love the world's ways and are afraid or unwilling to give them up for something better. There are things about the world that are fun and exciting. You might be worried you'll exchange a fun and exciting life without limits for a boring one. You might be clinging on to a toxic relationship because you're afraid to be single when God has someone so much better in store for you. You might be hanging on to your addiction when Jesus is offering you a new life of freedom. What are you hanging on to, afraid to give up because you don't trust that God has something more for you?

As women, we are created for greatness and depth. I love these words attributed to Ann Voskamp: "Please hear me, Girl: The world has enough women who know how to do their hair. It needs women who know how to do hard and holy things."[1] On social media, there is no shortage of people broadcasting their every latte, new outfit, workout, and plate of avocado toast. All these things can be fun, but as women of God, we've been called to do hard and holy things of eternal value. We haven't been made to stare at our phones for hours a day just to watch other people's lives unfold through staged and filtered photos and videos. We've been called to live our own lives. Our actual lives. We are called to be instruments of mercy and kindness. And there is nothing boring about being used by God. As we turn our gaze away from the empty ways of this world, we discover a greater calling. We are invited into a story so much bigger than ourselves.

Being made for more means choosing the better thing even when you're being tempted by the world's distractions. We see this in the life of a woman named Mary, sister of Martha and Lazarus. Mary and Martha had opened their home to Jesus as He was traveling with His disciples. Martha busied herself with preparations while Mary sat at Jesus' feet listening to His words of wisdom. Frustrated with Mary, Martha says to Jesus, "Lord, don't you care that my sister has left me to do the work by myself? Tell her to help me!" Jesus replied, "Martha, Martha, . . .you are worried and upset about many things, but few things are needed—or indeed only one. Mary has chosen what is better, and it will not be taken away from her" (Luke 10:40–42).

Choosing God above all else means choosing what is better. It means living a better life. I believe Martha had good intentions. I think she loved Jesus dearly and this motivated her desire to serve Him the best she could. Unfortunately, she became anxious with the tasks in front of her and was consumed by lesser things. This led her to miss what she was made for—being fully present with the Creator and Savior of the world.

Martha also lost herself in the dangerous trap of comparison, and it stole her joy. It seems she was resentful at her sister and this made her bitter. How often do we allow busyness, comparison, and striving to cheat us out of the life of peace and presence we've been made for? Mary chose presence over distraction. She chose to sit at the feet of the God who created her and the only One who could fill every void in her life. She worshiped instead of worried and in Jesus' presence found the fullness of joy.

As you continue or embark on your journey toward a life of more, let this be your prayer: "Turn my eyes from worthless things and give me life through your word" (Psalm 119:37 NLT). What are the things in your life that King Solomon would call "meaningless, a chasing after the wind" (Ecclesiastes 1:14)? What is undeserving of your one beautiful and precious life? What habits, relationships, and addictions are keeping you from living the life you've been made for?

With God as your helper, you have the strength and courage to walk away from the things that jeopardize your true value and purpose. A greater life is ahead than the life we leave behind. When you hand God the tattered things you've been clinging to, He exchanges them for something far better. Are you ready to let go and let God do a new thing in your life?

Be Still and Be Loved

A TIME TO REFLECT

What is keeping you from living a life of deep purpose and significance?

God,
Help me release the things that are keeping me from Your best for me. Help me trust that Your path is better than the world's way. Empower me to choose presence over distraction and discover the fullness of joy.

10

Made to Live Forever

She was made for more than what her eyes can see.

As we go about our days, life can seem permanent. It is easy to take it for granted. We sometimes feel like this earth is our forever home and that we'll always be here. But when we unexpectedly lose someone we love, we are reminded that life is fragile and fleeting. Death reminds us of our own mortality—that we can't escape it and one day it will come for us.

David, the psalmist, asked God to impress on him the brevity of life: "Show me, LORD, my life's end and the number of my days; let me know how fleeting my life is. You have made my days a mere handbreadth; the span of my years is as nothing before you.

Everyone is but a breath, even those who seem secure" (Psalm 39:4–5). In the grand scheme of eternity, our lives here in this broken world are a vapor. "What is your life? You are a mist that appears for a little while and then vanishes" (James 4:14). This world is all we know, but this world is not all there is. Though our life on earth is temporary, God places immense value on our lives, so much so that He made us to live forever in eternity with Him.

Not only are we quick to forget how fragile our life is, we also experience a homesickness for heaven. C. S. Lewis said, "If I find in myself a desire which no experience in this world can satisfy, the most probable explanation is that I was made for another world."[1]

Even on our best days, we fail to find supreme happiness in this life. We know in the core of our being there is something more—something perfect and beautiful and whole. We think what we need is a new wardrobe, a nicer living space, a relationship, or our dream job, but it's heaven our weary souls are searching for.

God made us for forever: "He has also set eternity in the human heart; yet no one can fathom what God has done from beginning to end" (Ecclesiastes 3:11). In our spirit, we know we've been created for everlasting life. We can't begin to imagine the scope of God's eternal story and all that is ahead.

There are only two destinations we can spend eternity in—heaven or hell, and Jesus teaches about them both. In his book *Heaven,* Randy Alcorn explains what our life on earth also teaches us about them.

Earth is an in-between world touched by both Heaven and Hell. Earth leads directly into Heaven or directly into Hell, affording a choice between the two. The best of life on Earth is a glimpse of Heaven; the worst of life is a glimpse of Hell.[2]

God is righteous and holy, and sin and brokenness have no dominion or presence in heaven. Jesus teaches that our sins call for eternal judgment in hell, but that through His grace, those who believe in Him have a path to complete forgiveness and everlasting life. If you reject God's love and the gift of salvation, you will spend eternity apart from Him. It is up to us to receive the gift of eternal life. Be reminded of this: "For God so loved the world that he gave his one and only Son, that whoever believes in him shall not perish but have eternal life" (John 3:16).

Have you made peace with God? Do you have confidence that you will spend eternity with Him in heaven? If you have not, turn to the end of this book. There you will find a prayer to guide you as you make the most important decision of your life by surrendering your life to Christ.

We know we've been made to live forever, but what is heaven really like? Will we just spend eternity in a holy trance singing hymns and worship songs? Not at all. Though the mystery of heaven has yet to be unveiled to us, it will be more incredible than we can possibly imagine: "'What no eye has seen, what no ear has heard, and what no human mind has conceived'—the things God has prepared for those who love him" (1 Corinthians 2:9).

God will make a new heaven and new earth (Revelation 21:1). It will be more beautiful than we can fathom and we will experience it with our new heavenly bodies and all our senses. There will be laughter, reunions with loved ones, dazzling beauty, celebration, and healing.

The Bible teaches that Jesus will wipe every tear from our eyes and that "there will be no more death or mourning or crying or pain, for the old order of things has passed away" (Revelation 21:4). In heaven, there will be no need for hospitals, cemeteries, or prisons. Fear, grief, and pain will have no place in eternity.

Our restored heavenly bodies will be free from sickness and shame. It is in heaven that we will finally discover our complete identity. We will finally truly be ourselves, unencumbered by our shortcomings and addictions. We will be free to be the women we've been designed to be—whole, complete, and more alive than ever.

When we believe our citizenship is in heaven (Philippians 3:20), it changes the way we live. When life falls apart around us, we have an eternal hope that cannot be shaken. A foolish woman has never learned to number her days. A wise woman knows her days on earth are few but that she has been made for so much more than she can see: "The world and its desires pass away, but whoever does the will of God lives forever" (1 John 2:17).

> **When life falls apart around us, we have an eternal hope that cannot be shaken.**

Choose to live your life with passion and intention, but cultivate an eternal perspective: "So we fix our eyes not on what is seen, but on what is unseen, since what is seen is temporary, but what is unseen is eternal" (2 Corinthians 4:18). God has made you to live forever because He loves you. Your home is securely established in heaven if you have surrendered your life to Christ. With faith, this gift will never be taken away: "I give them eternal life, and they shall never perish; no one will snatch them out of my hand" (John 10:28).

Countless hymns and songs celebrate heaven. The hymn "Eternity" by Will L. Thompson invites us to choose heaven:

Where spend eternity
When earth is gone?
Where will my spirit be
As time goes on?
Earth's pleasures cannot stay,
Soon, soon they pass away,
Then comes the long, long day,
Eternity.

Choose now thy future home,
Choose weary soul,
Where thro' eternity
Ages may roll.
Serve faithfully while here,
Bring Christ some souls to cheer,
Love God, then never fear,
Eternity.[3]

God's loving purpose for your life does not end the day your heart stops beating. If you are in Christ, that is when it truly begins. When the troubles of this world seem to overtake you, be still. Jesus is ready to comfort you: "Do not let your hearts be troubled. You believe in God; believe also in me. My Father's house has many rooms; if that were not so, would I have told you that I am going there to prepare a place for you? And if I go and prepare a place for you, I will come back and take you to be with me that you also may be where I am. You know the way to the place where I am going" (John 14:1–4). There is a room waiting for you if you want it. Will you receive the gift of your eternal home?

Be Still and Be Loved

A TIME TO REFLECT

How can you live a life of purpose on earth while keeping a heavenly perspective?

Jesus,
Thank You that You have set eternity in my heart and that You have gone to prepare a place for me. Teach me to number my days. Help me be faithful with the life You have given me and thank You that one day You will wipe away all my tears.

11

Made to Live Fearlessly

Overcome by a perfect love, she's no longer ruled by fear.

One of my greatest passions is surfing. Drenched in saltwater, I feel whole and free—fully alive, as dolphins glide by me and the sun slips below the endless sea. Unlike basketball or soccer or most sports, surfing presents the rare but real possibility that you may come face to face with a great white shark. As a surfer, the threat is real. There have been two fatal attacks near our home, and we know shark attack survivors personally. One day my husband and I were surfing a beach break in Santa Cruz while, unbeknownst to us, a twenty-six-year-old surfer was fatally attacked just a quarter mile away. While we avoid spots that we know are extra "sharky," we continue to paddle out because our passion for riding waves is greater than our fear of what's lurking beneath the surface.

While sharks might not keep me out of the water, I have battled fear, worry, and at times anxiety for other reasons. In college, there was a season where I would get unexplained panic attacks. Right before I would fall asleep, my body would become paralyzed and I couldn't breathe. I thought I was dying. The first time it happened I woke my resident advisor in tears—traumatized and terrified. While anxiety and panic attacks are very real mental health issues that can be treated with professional help, we have not been made to live in fear.

Fear is a basic human emotion. It is a necessary survival instinct that can keep us safe. Fear can inform us and help us make wise choices. In the Bible, God makes it clear that we are to cast our fear upon Him. God understands our fear, but calls us to live fearlessly and trust that He is in control of our lives. "Fear not" is the most repeated command in the Bible, appearing at least eighty times.

The world can be a scary place. We have much to be concerned about. We face the threat of natural disasters, wars, pandemics, health crises, financial trials, and the loss of people we love, to name a few. Writer and theologian Frederick Buechner said, "Here is the world. Beautiful and terrible things will happen. Don't be afraid."[1] Jesus lovingly told us, "So don't be afraid; you are worth more than many sparrows" (Matthew 10:31). In this verse, I believe Jesus is saying, "I love you and I've got you. You are of immense value to me and I will fight for you." Jesus also reminds us, "Who of you by worrying can add a single hour to your life?" (Luke 12:25). God did not intend for us to live our days preoccupied with anxiety and worry. He made us for greater things. Above all, He made us to be loved by Him. Remember, "There is no fear in love. But perfect love drives out fear" (1 John 4:18). Hide yourself in the love of Christ where fear is overcome.

In Matthew 14:22–31, we are given a great example of the importance of keeping our eyes on Jesus during difficult times. The disciples were on a boat when a storm surrounded them. Jesus, who was on the mountainside alone praying, entered the storm and began to walk on water toward the boat. When the disciples saw Him, they were terrified and thought He was a ghost. As the storm swirled around them, Jesus said, "Take courage! It is I. Don't be afraid" (Matthew 14:27). Knowing it was Jesus, Peter got out of the boat and walked on the water toward Him. As the wind intensified, Peter was enveloped by fear and took his eyes off Jesus. He cried out, "Lord, save me!" (Matthew 14:30). Jesus reached out His hand and caught Peter, saying, "You of little faith, why did you doubt?" (Matthew 14:31).

Jesus didn't cause the storm to end, He overpowered it. He entered the storm and was present in it with His disciples whom He loved. God might not take your storm away, but He promises to be with you in it, even when you don't sense His presence. I love the illustration of Peter keeping his eyes fixed on Jesus as the seas roared and the wind swirled around him. I know I need to keep my eyes on God, not the difficult circumstances surrounding me.

God might not take your storm away, but He promises to be with you in it.

Keeping our eyes on Jesus in the middle of a storm shouldn't be just an abstract idea, but a practical strategy that will enable us to rise above the storms of our lives. While we can't control the intensity or duration of our storms, we do, like Peter, have the freedom to decide what we focus on.

Research has shown that frequent exposure to the news and social media significantly increases levels of anxiety. It is unnatural for us to know all the bad things that are happening around the world and what friends and strangers are doing 24/7. If we limit our exposure to these things, we can invest that mental energy in more positive ways and focus on our center of influence. In addition to limiting negative inputs, some tools for navigating storms and fighting anxiety include frequent prayer, Scripture meditation, counseling, journaling, singing hymns and spiritual songs, immersing yourself in healthy community, and asking others to pray for you. When I am anxious, I also practice deep breathing and grounding techniques that help me engage my senses, calm down, and focus on the present.

In times of fear or uncertainty, hide your face in the book of Psalms. Make the psalmist's prayers your prayers.

Psalm 56:3–4 says:

> When I am afraid, I put my trust in you.
>   In God, whose word I praise—
> In God I trust and am not afraid.
>   What can mere mortals do to me?

The next time you find yourself being overtaken by your circumstances, fill in the blank in this line with whatever your fears may be and say it aloud:

"When I am afraid of _____, I will trust in You, O Lord."

Say this when you are afraid of being alone or abandoned. Repeat it when you are facing an unknown future or a mountain you don't think you can climb. If you focus on your circumstances, they will overpower you. Remember that Jesus has overcome your trials and storms. He is inviting you to trust in Him and to "cast all your anxiety on him because he cares for you" (1 Peter 5:7). Let this verse guide you in moments of anxiety: "Do not be anxious about anything, but in every situation, by prayer and petition, with thanksgiving, present your requests to God. And the peace of God, which transcends all understanding, will guard your hearts and your minds in Christ Jesus" (Philippians 4:6–7).

Take a moment to name your fears—the things you cannot control. Surrender them before God. Pray for His help to live fearlessly in the face of your battles and believe that you already have victory. Take heart. You are His, and He has overcome the world.

Be Still and Be Loved

A TIME TO REFLECT

What are your greatest fears and anxieties and what would it look like to entrust them to God?

Lord,
I choose to believe that You are fully present with me during my storms. Thank You that You have overcome not only my storms but the pain and brokenness of this world. Help me turn my eyes from my circumstances and focus on Your promises. Equip me with practical tools and strategies for fighting fear and anxiety. Give me the courage to live fearlessly as I trust You with my life.

12

Made to Walk Worthy

She's radiant.

Guilt is the feeling we experience after we do something wrong; shame is the belief that we are fundamentally wrong. To experience shame is to feel inadequate, insufficient, inferior, unworthy, and even unlovable. Shame says you aren't worthy of love or being known and accepted for who you really are. Too many girls and women are clothed in shame. Shame is often associated with mental health issues, but it is also universal. Shame is a pervasive part of the human experience, but it's not the identity God invites us to live into.

Shame was not part of God's design for us. We were made to live in a world where we are loved and free. After God created

Adam and Eve, they lived naked and unashamed (Genesis 2:25). They were fully known by God and at peace with God and themselves. God gave Adam and Eve the freedom to delight in all He had made and to choose to obey or not His one rule—not to eat the forbidden fruit. After Eve rebelled and took that first bite, shame entered the human story.

They became ashamed of their nakedness, which caused them to run for cover from God, sewing fig leaves together to hide beneath. We've been hiding ever since. Some of us hide with perfectionism and people pleasing. Others hide behind self-destructive addictions and behaviors that reinforce the lies we believe about ourselves. We might hide through shallow relationships. How has shame or the belief you are unworthy of love and community made you hide?

Shame has many origins. We can feel covered with shame when we sin or fall short of God's standards for our lives. *You slept with that boy. You partied until you passed out and did something stupid.* There's the shame inflicted on us by the words and actions of others. *He touched you where he shouldn't have and in ways that were wrong. She betrayed you and walked away from your friendship.* There's shame inflicted by Satan, the father of lies, who tells you untrue things so convincingly. *You will never overcome this. This world doesn't need you.* There's shame from the culture we live in. *You must look like her to be worthy of love. You must have a following to be significant.*

In its most dangerous form, shame can become a pervading experience, shaping your every thought and action. It can cause you to make destructive decisions that further reinforce your sense of unworthiness. Too many of us spend our lives devoid of the security and joy God desires for us because of shame. Thankfully, whatever its origin, shame does not have to be your destiny. The shameful parts of your past have no credible place in your present or future. Your mistakes, failures, and breakdowns don't deserve a role in the beautiful unfolding of what is yet to come.

Jesus is the lifter of our shame. We see this truth played out through His many encounters with outcasts, sinners, and the sick. Having met Jesus, they did not leave the same as they came. As Jesus was traveling to a man's home to heal his dying daughter, a woman consumed with shame as a result of uncontrollable bleeding for twelve years lunged from a crowd and touched Jesus' garment. She thought, "If I just touch his clothes, I will be healed" (Mark 5:28). She was right, and immediately, she was healed. Jesus knew that power had gone out from Him and asked, "Who touched my clothes?" The woman "came and fell at his feet and, trembling with fear, told him the whole truth" (Mark 5:33). Jesus said to her, "Daughter, your faith has healed you. Go in peace and be freed from your suffering" (Mark 5:34).

This woman's physical condition made her "unclean" according to Jewish law. She was forced to live as an outcast, alone and isolated. Even though her condition had worsened, this woman hadn't lost hope. She sought out Jesus with a heart full of hope, believing He could heal her. After Jesus asked who had touched Him, the woman came forward, afraid. Would she be in trouble? Would Jesus take back her healing? It took faith to reach out and touch Jesus, and it took courage to step forward from the crowd and admit she was the one who touched Him. There, Jesus spoke one word that changed everything. He called her "daughter." With this she was not only healed and made clean, she received eternal love, belonging, and a brand new identity.

Psalm 34:5 beautifully says, "Those who look to him are radiant; their faces are never covered with shame." Allow God to be the lifter of your shame. While Satan is the master shame artist, Jesus is our shame lifter. The bleeding woman was not the same when she left Jesus' presence. He exchanged the name "outcast" for "daughter." What is the shame story of your life? What untrue names and lies does Jesus want to remove in your life and replace with what is true and will set you free?

When we "take off" our old selves or who we've been apart from God and clothe ourselves in our new identity, shame dissipates and we rise to live in freedom and radiance. Shame comes from looking inward and outward. A radiant woman looks up to God for her worth, rather than to herself or others. We can't make ourselves radiant. We have no light of our own. But the more we delight ourselves in God, the more His light overtakes us and consumes our darkness and emptiness. Just as the bleeding woman sought out Jesus, we must make the deliberate choice to position ourselves directly in front of His contagious radiance.

> **But when we position ourselves in front of the radiance of the Son (Jesus), much like the moon does for the earth, we reflect His light and our shame is overwhelmed by love.**

While it's Jesus who perfectly radiates the glory of God, we are to reflect His glory to the world. He is the big, true light; we are the little lights. It's like the sun and the moon. We are captivated by the beauty and brightness of a full moon, but the moon has no light of its own. Apart from the sun, it's just a dark, empty rock floating in space. In the same way, without God, we are in darkness, consumed by unworthiness. But when we position ourselves in front of the radiance of the Son (Jesus), much like the moon does for the earth, we reflect His light and our shame is overwhelmed by love.

Not only does God want to be the lifter of our shame, He wants to use us to erase unworthiness in other people's lives. We get to be women who speak truth into the lives of family, friends, and even strangers. We get to invite them into a new identity and point them to the One who speaks worth and value over them.

We are called to "live a life worthy of the calling you have received" (Ephesians 4:1). This means you are invited to act in a way that reflects the goodness of God and the life of purpose He has for you. Because of your faith, shame no longer has any place in your story. Ask God to give you wisdom as you seek the origin of shame in your life. Ask Him to give you an anthem of truth to drown out the lies that have made you a prisoner to shame in your own life. Position yourself in His radiance where lies and unworthiness cannot exist. You are His daughter. You are worthy of love and you belong.

Be Still and Be Loved

A TIME TO REFLECT

How can you allow God to be the lifter of your shame?

Lord,
Be the lifter of my shame. Heal my unworthiness with Your love. Help me stop hiding and give me the courage to walk worthy of the calling I have received. Silence the lies shame tells me, and make me radiant as I look to You.

13

Made to Be Redeemed

He traded her ashes for beauty.

*I*n Japanese culture, there is a type of pottery known as Kintsugi or Kintsukuroi. It is the art of repairing broken pottery with a lacquer mixed with powdered gold, silver, or platinum.[1] The once-present cracks from being shattered are mended and then accentuated with the lacquer. Rather than the breakage being undesirable, the cracks instead are emphasized as part of the object's history while making it even more beautiful. The philosophy of Kintsugi is an analogy of what God can do with our broken lives.

God is the potter: "Yet you, LORD, are our Father. We are the clay, you are the potter; we are all the work of your hand" (Isaiah

64:8). Even when we break or come undone, we are never too far from being mended. To be in our potter's hands is the safest place to be.

In breaking and coming to God, we become more beautiful. God can redeem the broken parts of our lives and put us back together stronger than we were before. Christ's restorative power that has overcome death mends the places where we are crushed, making us whole to shine like gold.

Redemption means to take back or buy back. It is "the action of saving or being saved from sin, error, or evil" and "the action of regaining or gaining possession of something in exchange for payment, or clearing a debt."[2] Jesus has come to save us from sin and evil and to replace the most broken parts of our lives with beauty and purpose.

> **In breaking and coming to God, we become more beautiful.**

God has cleared our debt: "I have swept away your offenses like a cloud, your sins like the morning mist. Return to me, for I have redeemed you" (Isaiah 44:22). God has a plan to redeem this decaying world and offers the gift of redemption to His children as they place their faith in Christ. Redemption is the reversal of everything that's gone wrong in our personal lives and in this fallen world.

It's often the things the world tells us we should hide that have the potential to be used by God in ways you could never imagine. During treatment for my mental health challenges, I never imagined a way forward or that any good could come from being so broken. As I packed my bag for that psychiatric hospital two weeks after graduating high school, I thought my life was over. I believed I would never make it out of those four walls. However, in God's miraculous way, my life has been restored and I have even found good gifts from coming apart. God has taken all the shattered pieces of my life and mended them. And He's done this for me more than once. With God, our wounds can be healed and used for good. Even the terrible things that have been done to us can be redeemed.

My friend Tammy was a victim of sex trafficking as a girl. She has seen God take the wounds she experienced from years of abuse and victimization and give her healing and purpose. Tammy was born in Hawaii, abandoned by her mother at the age of three months, and taken in by a man who was not her father. "From the time I was four years old, I remember him sexually abusing me," she said. Not knowing it was wrong, she didn't tell anyone until she was thirteen. Child Protective Services was notified, and Tammy was eventually put into foster care. However, she didn't receive counseling or treatment for the abuse and she became promiscuous and began to drink alcohol and use drugs.

While in foster care, Tammy met a girl who had been working with a pimp and made the sex industry sound glamorous. "I met a pimp on the beach in Waikiki and ended up working for him," she said. "I was under his control for five months. I then went back into foster care, and two years later, I became a teen mom at the age of eighteen and began street walking to provide for my son." She was in and out of this lifestyle until her thirties.

A concerned friend invited Tammy to church, warning her that if she didn't turn her life around, she might die. As broken as could be, Tammy heard the gospel, gave her life to Christ, and over time, the Holy Spirit began to radically transform her life, making her brand new.

Today, Tammy is the advocate and outreach coordinator for an organization that fights child sex trafficking and provides care for children who have been exploited. Tammy works with victimized children and adults and offers insight and expertise that can only come from being a survivor of childhood sexual exploitation. Tammy's life is a testament to how God can redeem evil and abuse in our lives.

Maybe, like me, you have come apart, or maybe, like Tammy, you have been a victim of evil; but by coming to God, the broken parts of your life can be mended. In offering your shattered life to God, you can be made—like a piece of Kintsugi pottery—not just whole but more beautiful. The cracks and crevices of our lives are a part of our stories, but they aren't the end of our stories. They are a part of us, but they do not define who we are.

Our struggles are not our identities. We are defined by the love of Christ that picks up our broken pieces, mends us, and makes us lovelier than before, lovelier than what we ever envisioned. It's the imperfect parts of our lives that draw us to one another. Perfectionism separates us but it's our collective brokenness that connects us in this hard world and shows our need for a Savior.

God has this message for you: "Do not fear, for I have redeemed you; I have summoned you by name; you are mine" (Isaiah 43:1). God is going to use all this pain for good. Somehow, though it might take a while, in His perfect time, in this world or in eternity, your broken pieces will be mended into something beautiful. And even if you shatter again, God will mend you again over and over.

As His workmanship, God's eternal plan for you is good. Sometimes we experience our mending on this side of eternity.

Sometimes we just get glimpses of it in this life. But if we don't, we know it is coming in heaven and that one day every tear will be wiped away (Revelation 21:4). There will be no more mourning, no more death or loss or heartache. Restoration, healing, and wholeness are coming. Do not let your heart be troubled. God is mending you. He is the Kintsugi artist and you are being fashioned for good.

Be Still and Be Loved

A TIME TO REFLECT

How can you surrender the broken parts of your life to Christ?

God,
Thank You that You refuse to leave me broken and detached from relationship with You. Thank You that You have redeemed the areas where I have fallen short and that You promise to bring good from the hard parts of my life and the things that have been done to me. I choose to trust that in Your perfect time, You will mend every shattered piece of my life and bring beauty from brokenness.

14

Made to Belong

She is finding new spaces where she can be loved and be free.

I've always wanted a close tribe of girlfriends to do life with, but I've never found or really been a part of a life-long "squad." During college, after my plans of playing soccer fell through, my roommates convinced me to participate in a sorority "rush" or recruitment process. I wore my best clothes and put my best face forward as I mingled with girls from each sorority chapter during rush week. I tried to be as impressive and charming as I could during these "auditions." I learned that after each night of recruitment the sorority members would rank and assess each girl and vote on whether she should be let into their sisterhood. Some of my roommates were devastated when, on the final night, they were not selected but received only rejection letters. I was selected but ended up joining reluctantly, unsure what my experience would be like. And though I made some treasured friends I am still connected with, I eventually dropped out because I felt God calling me to create a community that was not selective but inclusive.

While there can be some great things about sororities, it bothered me that everything about the system seemed so opposite to how God interacts with us. He doesn't require that we pay dues to be a part of His family, He doesn't rank us in preferential order, and we don't have to audition to be a part of His club.

Later that year, I started a campus club that I called—you guessed it—Wonderfully Made. Every woman was welcome to join. There was no recruitment process or dues. I put up a poster in the women's bathroom casting the vision for the group and three women came to our first meeting. Our small group of four grew into a loving sisterhood of over forty women and spread to three other campuses in California where women were given a place to belong. We had beach days, went on hikes, hosted game nights and dinner parties, and most importantly, gathered together to read the Bible and talk about God and our lives. Many of the women became one another's bridesmaids and are close friends to this day. Though it has evolved, this club was the beginning of the ministry I still direct today.

This world can be cold and lonely. Maybe you come from a broken home or struggle to find a place where you fit in, a place where you are loved and accepted. Maybe your days are filled with an inescapable loneliness. Our world is hyperconnected yet more isolating than ever. One fifteen-year-old girl I mentored showed me an app that constantly displayed her friends' locations. While we were talking over coffee, her friends were hanging out together and she hadn't been invited. It hurts to be excluded and made to feel as if we don't belong.

My friend Lily was put up for adoption at five weeks old into a family with two boys. Her birth parents had just graduated from high school and felt they were too young to raise her. Lily said, "As a girl, I often wondered about my birth family and why I was placed for adoption. Around the age of nine, my adopted dad began sexually abusing me, and I suffered emotional abuse from my adopted mom." Though Lily was secretly experiencing abuse in her home, her family took her to church every week. "At church I felt loved, safe, and significant. Church became my family."

Lily continued to suffer deep trauma, including the loss of a dear friend in a car accident. Lily turned away from God and searched for love and belonging in the wrong places, including a failed relationship. With time, she expressed her anger to God and restored her relationship with Him. Years later, motivated by a desire to learn more about her medical history, she took a DNA test. "My results astonishingly led me to find and be reunited with my birth family. They embraced me and told me they had always loved me and prayed for me."

As an adult, Lily's birth parents officially adopted her back into their family. "Though my journey hasn't been easy, and it's been hard to know where I fit in at times, God has always provided me with a sense of belonging and has given me a loving family."

Today, Lily is using her life's story to create a sense of belonging among the youth in her church. She is passionate about giving them a place to be a part of and reminding them that first and foremost they belong to God.

Our sense of not fitting in can often be the very thing God uses to draw us to a personal relationship with Him. Jesus invited men, women, children, Jews, Gentiles (people who were not Jewish), and everyone He encountered to be a part of something bigger than themselves. He invited them to be loved by Him and to be a part of the kingdom of God. We belong to God, and as believers, we belong to one another: "There is neither Jew nor Greek, there is neither slave nor free, there is no male and female, for you are all one in Christ Jesus" (Galatians 3:28 ESV). For the apostle Paul to say that we are all one in Christ was radical. Jews and Gentiles were intensely divided, and women then did not experience the freedom, respect, or equality to the degree we do today in our Western culture. In Jesus, the outcasts, the marginalized, and the successful all find a home and walk on equal ground.

> **Our sense of not fitting in can often be the very thing God uses to draw us to a personal relationship with Him.**

Two thousand years later, we still often fail to see one another as equals and are quick to put each other into categories. The two main categories we toss one another into are "like me" and "not like me." We are hesitant to associate with anyone different than us; but as believers, we are all one in Christ. The apostle Paul reminded us how much God desires equality and unity among His children. In days of fierce divisions, this is still God's heart. There is no black or white, male or female, rich or poor. We are equal before God, and we all have a seat at the table. We are given this instruction: "Live in harmony with one another. Do not be proud, but be willing to associate with people of low position.

Do not be conceited" (Romans 12:16).

Not only are we made to belong, we are made to create spaces for others to belong. The church is called to create this environment for everyone, and God expects us to rise to this challenge individually as well: "Offer hospitality to one another without grumbling" (1 Peter 4:9).

When is the last time you experienced genuine hospitality that made you feel welcome and loved? Who was the person offering you this hospitality? Ask God to cultivate a hospitable heart in you too. Ask Him to show you who He wants you to include and invite into community. Dream about what this community might look like—from a hiking group or book club to a Bible study or regular dinner gathering. So many are just waiting for an invitation to belong somewhere. Be the woman who extends the invitation.

Relationships can be messy. We are broken people and fall short of the way God desires us to live. Eventually, we will be hurt or disappointed by our family, friends, or church. When this happens, draw near to God in your pain and ask Him to teach you how to forgive. God remains steadfast and trustworthy even when people let us down. As messy as it can be, community and belonging are always worth fighting for: "Above all, keep loving one another earnestly, since love covers a multitude of sins" (1 Peter 4:8 ESV). We are made to belong to God and each other. Be an instrument God uses to create community and belonging in your sphere of influence as you find your true home in Him.

Be Still and Be Loved

A TIME TO REFLECT

Where can I experience deeper belonging and how can I create space for others to belong?

God,
Thank You that first and foremost I belong to You as Your daughter. Use my loneliness to draw me closer to You, and please show me where I belong in this world. Give me the community I crave. Help me have a hospitable heart and create spaces for others to feel known, welcome, and loved. Help me not grow bitter when I am hurt by others. Instead, teach me to forgive and love others as You call me to do.

15

Made for Friendship

In her presence, you are always enough and never too much.

*E*very little girl wishes for a best friend. Someone to have endless adventures and playdates with. Someone to safely tell her secrets to and whose friendship she can have all to herself. The funny thing I've learned is even when we grow up and are no longer little girls, we still want a best friend, and we want everyone to know we have one. There is a security and sense of worth that comes with having that "bff" or best friend forever.

My childhood friend Kelly and I were inseparable. We joined tap, ballet, jazz, and art classes and played on the same soccer team as two of only three girls. We both had freckles and loved writing plays and performing for Kelly's dog. In Kelly's presence, I felt known and secure and as though I belonged to someone. This is the gift authentic friendship can bring, and as women, it is still the desire of our heart.

As we get older, change, and enter different chapters of our lives, we often drift away from the friends we once held so dear. Friendships, like family relationships, can be messy and complicated. Drama sometimes unfolds, and we can get hurt. In high school, I was sometimes wounded by friends and was encircled by drama (usually concerning boys) as is a common experience for many girls.

Proverbs 16:28 tells us that "gossip separates close friends." I don't know if gossip exists anywhere like it does in the halls of junior highs and high schools, but unfortunately gossiping women don't become extinct after high school graduation. There are plenty of gossipy women in sororities, churches, and mom groups. When you're getting to know someone new and she starts speaking negatively about someone in front of you, ditch your latte and run for the door! Now is the time to get out before she starts talking smack about you.

The great thing about friendships is that God lets us decide who we want in our inner circle. We get to choose the people we do life with. As I got older and my relationship with God began to inform my every decision, I found friends who shared my faith and values and treated me with kindness and respect.

In college, I made one of my closest friends, Kayla. She later became the maid of honor at my wedding. When I started that campus club, Kayla was one of the three women who responded to the poster I put up in the women's bathroom. She helped launch the entire ministry of Wonderfully Made, and her radiant personality attracted the dozens of young women who became a part of our authentic community. She is still a faithful friend and mentor to many of these women today.

My friendship with Kayla was the first friendship I formed that wasn't somehow marred by drama. Fifteen plus years into our friendship and we still haven't had a fight. Yes, we've had things we've had to work through, but we have always treated each other with love and dignity. We have been able to live this verse out in our friendship: "Bear with each other and forgive one another if any of you has a grievance against someone. Forgive as the Lord forgave you" (Colossians 3:13).

If I'm being honest, the insecure girl in me would sometimes like to have Kayla all to myself, but being such an incredible person, she has an entire cheerleading squad of "best friends" whom she makes feel equally loved and special. I'm realizing this is the way it should be. I have come to believe that friendships that make others feel inferior or excluded aren't healthy and they aren't honoring to God. I like to call my closest friends my "treasured" friends because I treasure them each uniquely.

An authentic friend "loves at all times" (Proverbs 17:17). Kayla has seen me at my very worst and still loves me. She sees me for who I am, even when I've struggled. Even though we currently live on opposite coasts and our lives today couldn't look more different, we've made it a priority to invest in our friendship. Invest in people who treat you in a way that reflects God's love for you and hold on to them. Let this verse guide your friendships: "Therefore encourage one another and build each other up, just as in fact you are doing" (1 Thessalonians 5:11).

Ask God to show you how to be a good friend. Remember birthdays, send handwritten notes, honor confidentiality, listen intently, and love without condition. Be the kind of friend you want for yourself. If we want healthy relationships, the best thing we can do is become the healthiest versions of ourselves. Ask God to heal you emotionally so you can thrive in your friendships. Ask Him to use you to bring love and community to the lives of your friends.

Rather than always looking to receive, go into friendships with a heart to serve and encourage the other person. While serving your friends is important, at the same time healthy friendships are never one-sided. They should be reciprocal as each person invests energy and time into the relationship in a way that is mutual. If you find yourself constantly giving and investing in a friendship but the effort is never returned, it might be time to find new friendships that are honoring to you as well.

Go into friendships with a heart to serve and encourage the other person.

Authentic friendships don't age discriminate. Three of my most treasured friends are decades older than I am. One of my mentors recently turned eighty. Her mentoring presence in my life has brought me endless encouragement and wisdom. Mentors are wise friends who are like lighthouses, illuminating our path through seasons of uncertainty and darkness. Through their lives, they teach us more about the character of God and show us how to live wisely.

As we pursue God and walk on the road that leads to life, we are called to invest in the lives of girls and women younger than we are. This is a high calling. There will always be a lost and hurting generation in need of good role models to lead the way. Who is someone younger you can invest in and encourage?

Our friendships influence our future. Periodically, it is helpful to evaluate your friendships. Ask yourself if your friendships are moving you in a positive direction. Consider if they are drawing you closer to God or further away from Him. Take an honest account of your friendships and know that, when necessary, it is okay to gracefully distance yourself from someone. If it's clear a friendship in your life needs to end, try to go your separate ways on good terms by giving the relationship space to breathe. Sometimes, friendships can rekindle in the future, and other times you find yourself needing to walk away.

In the past, I have placed unrealistic expectations on a friend that were not fair to her and that she couldn't live up to. If you find yourself hurt from a friend, hide yourself in God and love her anyway. Be quick to offer forgiveness and ask God to examine your heart and to show you areas where you can grow. We will be let down by our friends, and we will let our friends down. Disappointments in friendships are an opportunity to turn to God. They remind us that no one person can be all things for us.

Let's be women who are so secure in our identity in Christ that we don't go to one person for our validation or sense of security, but are friendly to all. Let's rise to the challenge of learning how to be a loving and faithful friend. As you cultivate greater wholeness in your life and learn to be the kind of friend you desire to have yourself, you can experience the beautiful gift of authentic friendship that God desires you to have.

Be Still and Be Loved

A TIME TO REFLECT

In what ways can I become more emotionally healthy so I can be a better friend?

God,
Thank You for the gift of friendship. Teach me how to be a good friend and bless me with loving and trustworthy friends who I can journey through life with. Help me be a friend who loves at all times and is quick to forgive. Please give me wisdom in my relationships and help me cultivate life-giving friendships that are centered on You.

16

Made to Persevere

**Her joy is unshakable.
She will not be moved.**

As a young girl, I never experienced the harshness that life sometimes brings. I viewed my life and my future through rose-colored glasses. I had a loving family, everything I needed, a world of opportunity, and a house with a view where each night I would watch the sun slip beneath the horizon as my dog Sunny sat by my side. As the sun set, I would daydream about what I wanted my life to look like one day. In high school, fighting back what I now know was clinical depression, I pressed on toward the pursuit of my ideal life until I completely fell apart. My first taste of suffering shook me to the core, but it was the very thing that led me to God. This was the greatest gift among many that suffering has given me.

In this world, we will experience pain and suffering, and our white-picket-fence dreams don't always come true. Jesus told us we will have trouble (John 16:33). The plans we make for our lives can fall apart. We encounter unexpected detours that throw us off course. Loss and tragedy can strike at any moment. However, we must not live in fear, but rather believe God will give us the grace to endure. As hard as this life can be, good gifts can be found in suffering, and joy and pain can coexist.

The idea that joy can only be found in a pain-free life is a lie. No one I know exposes this lie more than my friend Katherine Wolf. At the age of twenty-six, Katherine suffered a massive brain stem stroke that almost killed her. She underwent a sixteen-hour surgery that saved her life, but left her with severe disabilities. Still today, she can't drive a car or walk unassisted. She uses a wheelchair, and one side of her face is paralyzed. Pain and struggle is an everyday part of her life.

Despite this, Katherine and her family fight for joy every day, finding good gifts in hard places. Katherine believes "suffering isn't the end of the story but the beginning of a new one." Reflecting on suffering, Katherine shared: "In our deepest darkest times, God is at work, and He's called us there to teach us important things that will inform the rest of our lives."

Katherine shares a unique perspective on our collective brokenness. She believes we are all wounded and walking around with what she calls "invisible wheelchairs," whether it's childhood trauma, shattered dreams, or mental illness. Katherine believes we are all suffering through various challenges and yet as believers "we share the same story of suffering and strength in Jesus."[1]

Whether she's speaking to a packed auditorium and making the room erupt in laughter, leading a camp for families affected by disabilities, doing a victory dance at her doctor's office after a good report, or eating a cupcake with delight, Katherine oozes joy. Her joy is a testament of hope that even in the hard places, God is still good and is at work.

We worship a Savior who has endured the greatest suffering in history, having been beaten, ridiculed, rejected, and crucified by the people He created and came to save. When we go through unbearable times of pain and sorrow, we can trust that Jesus understands our suffering and will help us endure our trials.

Have you experienced suffering in your life? Do you have an invisible wheelchair—a part of your life that has been marred by pain and struggle? The Bible teaches us about suffering with this challenge: "Consider it pure joy, my brothers and sisters, whenever you face trials of many kinds, because you know that the testing of your faith produces perseverance. Let perseverance finish its work so that you may be mature and complete, not lacking anything" (James 1:2–4). This verse reminds us that we are made to persevere through our trials as God uses them to refine us.

When making a piece of jewelry, a silversmith holds the piece of silver over the middle of a blazing fire where the flames are the hottest. Doing so burns away the impurities in the silver, simultaneously making the piece of silver stronger. The silversmith must sit in front of the fire as his work is purified and strengthened amidst the flames. He never takes his eyes off the silver, and if it is left in the flames too long, it will be destroyed. A silversmith knows a piece of silver is fully refined when he can see his reflection in it. Our sufferings can lead us to reflect Christ to the world.

When we walk through fires in our lives, God is our silver-smith: "He will sit as a refiner and purifier of silver" (Malachi 3:3). God is our loving, faithful, and ever-present refiner. He never abandons us in times of great suffering. When we surrender in trust, the fire melts away impurities in our lives. As we persevere through faith, God sees His reflection in us and we become more like Him. As believers, suffering does not go wasted: "We also glory in our sufferings, because we know that suffering produces perseverance; perseverance, character; and character, hope" (Romans 5:3–4).

As Katherine explained, suffering doesn't have to be the end of our story: "And the God of all grace, who called you to his eternal glory in Christ, after you have suffered a little while, will himself restore you and make you strong, firm and steadfast" (1 Peter 5:10). Sometimes we experience healing and deliverance from suffering here on earth, while other times, healing awaits us only in heaven. But no matter what, our tears are not wasted because God promises to restore us.

If all my dreams had come true, yes, I would have had an easy life so far. But I would have missed out on the treasures my pain and suffering have given me. I would lack depth and empathy. I would be spending my days in shallow living, self-absorbed and probably chasing after things of no lasting value. I wouldn't know joy the way it is meant to be experienced, and I would be missing out on deep friendship with God.

If you have experienced suffering and your life looks different than the way you once imagined it would, it's okay to be sad, to grieve, and to shed tears. It is okay to sit with your feelings and be angry or hurt. God can handle your emotions and wants an honest relationship with you. John Piper said, "Occasionally, weep deeply over the life that you hoped would be. Grieve the losses. Feel the pain. Then wash your face, trust God, and embrace the life that He's given you."[2]

In my life there have been long-held dreams that have never come to pass. Though I am grateful for the blessings and the story God has given me to live, there are also ways that my life looks very different from what I hoped for as a young girl. I have had to grieve the loss of these dreams over and over. Let the tears fall down your face for as long as they need to. And then when it's time, wash your face, arise to a new day, and bravely move forward into the story that is uniquely yours to live.

God doesn't send suffering to destroy us: "For our light and momentary troubles are achieving for us an eternal glory that far outweighs them all" (2 Corinthians 4:17). God has special blessings and honor for those who have endured the fire: "Blessed is the one who perseveres under trial because, having stood the test, that person will receive the crown of life that the Lord has promised to those who love him" (James 1:12).

With Jesus, our suffering isn't the end of the story. He will make the wrongs right; He will heal our hearts. He will one day give us a new heavenly body and redeem the pain we have experienced. Trust that God will help you persevere through any trial that comes your way and believe He is working all things together for good because He loves you and you have been called according to His purpose (Romans 8:28).

Be Still and Be Loved

A TIME TO REFLECT

How can you fight for joy in seasons of pain and struggle?

God,
I know that this world is broken and I will have trouble. Thank You that You have overcome the world. Carry me through any suffering I experience and help me persevere through my trials, trusting that my pain isn't the end of the story. Thank You that You promise to work all things together for my good and for Your glory. Thank You for making me to persevere.

17

Made for Such a Time as This

She's rising strong.

God saw you before you were born. All your days were written in His book before one of them ever came to be (Psalm 139:16). The exact day of your birth was no accident. You were made to exist at this exact time in history for a specific purpose. As I look back and reflect on the most well-known and influential women who ever lived, I realize that they were made to be alive and used by God for greatness at that specific time in history. Many of these women were brave and brilliant women of faith who faced unimaginable adversity and left legacies of greatness for us to learn from.

Susan B. Anthony was born in 1820 into a Quaker family in

Massachusetts. At the age of seventeen she collected anti-slavery petitions and went on to become a leading advocate for the abolition of slavery. She also dedicated her life to women's suffrage, a movement to give women the right to vote. She campaigned for women to own property, keep their income, and attend institutions of higher learning. Her work forever changed the future for women in America, and at the time of her death women in Wyoming, Utah, Colorado, and Idaho had received the right to vote.

Rosa Parks was born in 1913 and is known as the Mother of the Modern-Day Civil Rights Movement. She became famous when she peacefully refused to give up her seat to a white male on a bus, upholding the equal value and dignity of black men and women. In her book *Quiet Strength*, Rosa wrote, "I felt the Lord would give me the strength to endure whatever I had to face. God did away with all my fear. It was time for someone to stand up—or in my case, sit down. I refused to move."[1]

In the Old Testament book of Esther, we meet our unlikely heroine—a young Jewish orphan girl who rose in strength in the face of uncertain and terrifying times. After King Xerxes banished his wife Vashti from his kingdom for not performing scandalously at one of his parties, Esther was forced to compete for his attention in a beauty pageant of sorts with other virgins. Chosen for her beauty, she was given the new name Esther and was advised by her cousin and guardian Mordecai to keep her Jewish descent secret from the Persian king. The king's chief advisor Haman was offended by Mordecai and received permission from King Xerxes to kill the Jews. A genocide of Esther's people was about to happen.

Mordecai warned Esther, "For if you remain silent at this

time, relief and deliverance for the Jews will arise from another place, but you and your father's family will perish." He then said his famous words, "And who knows but that you have come to your royal position *for such a time as this*?" (Esther 4:14). Esther rose to the challenge, won the king's favor, and God used her to save the Jews.

God uses ordinary and unlikely people like an orphaned Jewish girl to do extraordinary things. Sometimes these extraordinary things begin with refusing to be silent, like Esther, on matters God cares about, such as human life, equality, poverty, abuse, and oppression. Esther was chosen by God. Just like her, you have been chosen to be an instrument of His love that helps bring the kingdom of God to earth.

As followers of Christ, we have a shared purpose to love people and to love God and make Him known. But you also have a unique call on your life that looks different from anyone else's. Frederick Buechner said, "The place God calls you to is

> **You also have a unique call on your life that looks different from anyone else's.**

the place where your deep gladness and the world's deep hunger meet."[2] What are the deep hungers or needs in the world around you that burden your heart? Your calling is where your burden meets your joy to serve and be used by God for good things.

Some of these divine assignments start movements, save lives, rescue the oppressed, and bring people into the kingdom of God. Jesus said, "The harvest is plentiful, but the laborers are few" (Matthew 9:37 ESV). God is always looking for women who will courageously answer the call He places on their lives.

Our calling is always greater than ourselves. Your call could be to become a wife and mother of future world-changers. It could be to serve at your local homeless shelter or as a youth leader in your church. Some of our divine assignments go unnoticed, while others will be recorded in history books. But none of them go unnoticed by God. God calls us all, but He calls us all differently.

Esther was faced with a choice. She could remain silent or rise strong in the face of terror and uncertainty. She unearthed the courage to do the hard thing. She wasn't looking to make history, but she was willing to be used by God, and in doing so, she forever changed the course of humanity. God used her to save an entire race of people.

We can be used by God right where we are with what we have. Esther used her beauty, position, and influence to rescue God's people. What is in you that God might want to use to accomplish worthwhile things? Is it your influence, education, or talents?

Esther moved forward through her fear. She might have done her assignment scared, but she did it. Susan B. Anthony and Rosa Parks experienced great resistance. Their passion for equality and what was right was greater than their fear. God gave them courage to gracefully push back against what they knew was wrong. Their bravery moved mountains and changed the future for generations to come.

Finding and answering our calling takes time and reflection. Esther fasted and prayed for three days before she bravely approached the king. An unexamined life of constant stimulation and distraction can keep us from discovering the life we've been made for. Have you ever set aside uninterrupted time to reflect on your life and ask God how He wants to use you? Consider planning a retreat for yourself where you get quiet and spend time examining your life. Ask God to show you the unique ways He wants to use you. Pray that, like Esther, you will have the courage to rise to the challenges in front of you with strength and dignity.

Just like Esther, Susan B. Anthony, and Rosa Parks, you have been made for such a time as this. Before you were created, God knew the exact time in history you would live. He knew the challenges you would face in your personal life and in the world. God is not surprised by the difficulties you face or the current events unfolding before you. You have been made for both beauty and hardship. You have not been made for an easy life. You haven't been made for a struggle-free life, but you have been made for such a time as this.

Be Still and Be Loved

A TIME TO REFLECT

Where does your "deep gladness and the world's deep hunger" meet?

God,
Thank You that You have made me for this time in history and that You want to use me to accomplish good things for Your glory. Help me discover the unique calling You have on my life. Give me courage in the face of adversity, and strengthen and equip me for the work You have called me to do.

18

Made for Soul Care

She treats herself with kindness and dignity.

What would your life look like five years from now if you began to care for yourself in a way that honors your God-given worth? We're not always the best at looking out for our own health and well-being. Sometimes, we can even be our own worst enemy. The driving reasons behind our lack of self-care are vast and varied, but can be tied to guilt, self-contempt, an overcrowded life, or a belief that we're unworthy of good things. The result can be poor mental and physical health that can keep us from living a rich and fulfilling life and doing the things we're called to do.

Self-care is all the rage, and the phrase has become a buzz

word. As women who seek to live for God and serve others, we might have a hard time justifying self-care without feeling selfish or guilty. With the right attitude and motivation, self-care is not selfish. It is not about self-indulgence; it is about stewardship. It is a way to honor God and be a good steward of the life He's given you: "Do you not know that your body is a temple of the Holy Spirit within you, whom you have from God? You are not your own, for you were bought with a price. So glorify God in your body" (1 Corinthians 6:19–20 ESV). But self-care is not just about caring for our bodies, or the outward parts of ourselves. It is also about caring for the inward parts of ourselves—our mind and spirit. So, self-care can be rightfully called "soul care."

> **We must learn to become a gentle and kind friend to ourselves.**

In a world where one in four adults suffer from a diagnosable mental disorder,[1] we must take responsibility for the way we care for ourselves. It's important that we learn to fight for our overall well-being by establishing rhythms and routines that promote vibrant emotional, physical, and spiritual health. If we want to be free, we must learn to become a gentle and kind friend to ourselves, treating ourselves with the same dignity with which we treat others.

We long to feel whole. When our lives are chaotic or disordered, it's hard to feel at peace with who we are. Too many of us are living at war with ourselves. This makes it hard to accomplish our goals and live into the unique purposes God has for us. While life is uncertain and we can't control a lot of what happens around us, we have more agency over our lives than we sometimes think. It's up to us to implement life-giving habits, routines, and practices into our lives and to vigilantly guard our health. No one else can do this for us and God wants to see us live at peace with ourselves.

Before we tackle the "how" or principles for soul care, it's important that we know our "why"—our motivation for greater wholeness. Why do you want to experience improved well-being? Why do you want to start taking better care of yourself? Knowing why will motivate us to put in the consistent effort needed to practice life-giving habits, rhythms, and routines.

My personal "why" for soul care is to be mentally and physically healthy so I can enjoy my life and be fully equipped to live out the purposes God has for me. This motivates me every day to get enough sleep and exercise, to take vitamins and medication, to feed my body with nourishing foods, to set aside quiet time, and to think true thoughts. I encourage you to write down your "why" as you take the next steps to nurture yourself in ways that honor God.

Living with a mental health condition for twenty years has forced me to take care of myself in this way. I know what it is like to break down and come apart and have to rebuild my life over and over. I have learned the hard way that stress, lack of sleep, negative thinking, hormonal and physiological imbalances, and poor habits can jeopardize my health. I have also learned many physical and spiritual disciplines that have helped to restore my health and enabled me to thrive and chase my dreams. As I guide you through some basic, well-known principles for good soul care, take time to reflect on your life and observe any areas of possible growth.

I believe that, apart from daily spending time with God, the most foundational thing we can do to care for ourselves is to get enough sleep. We spend one third of our lives sleeping. God wired the rhythm of rest and renewal into each day. "I lie down and sleep; I wake again, because the LORD sustains me" (Psalm 3:5). Set up your sleep for success. Tips for good sleep include going to bed and waking up at the same time, limiting your time on technology in the evening and keeping your phone away from your bed, making the environment in your bedroom conducive to good sleep, and avoiding caffeine later in the day. We simply can't function without adequate sleep. Good sleep enhances mood, increases productivity, reduces stress, and improves health.

Building upon the foundation of sleep is the habit of regular exercise. You don't need me to repeat the endless benefits of exercise, but I do want to ask: Are you regularly moving your body? Are you moving it in ways that bring you joy or are you in bondage to an unpleasant, rigid fitness routine? Explore many different activities such as walking, tennis, fitness classes, or cycling until you find the activities you enjoy the most. Invite a friend to join you as that always makes it more fun.

If you haven't already guessed what's next, what and how we eat are essential to our health and well-being. Food is nourishment and medicine. Much like our relationships with our bodies, our relationship with food can be chaotic, disordered, and complicated. I've been both underweight and very overweight. I know what it's like to be in bondage to disordered eating, dieting, bingeing, and poor body image. I also know that freedom is possible. Millions of girls and women suffer from life-threatening eating disorders. You might be one of them. God desires that we find balance and make peace with food. One thing you can do is pray over this area of your life. Invite God into the center of your relationship with food and ask Him to heal any unhealthy patterns and show you how to interact with food in a balanced and healthy way. If your relationship with food is disordered and unhealthy, seek professional help.

The next foundational step to excellent soul care is training our minds to think true and positive thoughts: "Finally, brothers and sisters, whatever is true, whatever is noble, whatever is right, whatever is pure, whatever is lovely, whatever is admirable—if anything is excellent or praiseworthy—think about such things" (Philippians 4:8). Memorize verses and truth declarations—such as "I am a child of God" or "my worth comes from God alone"—and repeat them throughout the day. Also, learn to identify any lies you are believing and combat them with truth.

There are many other habits and practices that promote well-being. What restores and replenishes you? Soul care can be simple things like taking a long walk, saying no to an opportunity, reading a book, writing in your journal, taking a bath, listening to music, and enjoying undistracted and intentional time alone.

But soul care isn't always bubble baths and instrumental music. Sometimes soul care can be cleaning physical clutter from your living space so you can have greater peace of mind. Sometimes it's having a difficult conversation with a friend or relative so you can protect your boundaries. Most importantly, soul care is partnering with God by asking Him to show you how to treat yourself in a way that affirms the worth He's created in you.

Be gentle with yourself on this journey toward taking better care of yourself. Ask God to teach you how to be a loving friend to yourself and to enjoy your own company. Be encouraged that with time you can feel more at peace with God and yourself. Soul care is about glorifying God with your life, learning to be at peace with yourself, and being fully equipped to live into your calling.

Be Still and Be Loved

A TIME TO REFLECT

What are three ways I can begin to practice better soul care?

God,
I ask that You help me take better care of myself. Help me show myself the same grace and compassion You show me. Teach me how to implement life-giving habits and routines into my life. Keep me mentally and physically healthy so I can live into the purposes You have for me.

19

Made to Create

She contributes and creates more than she consumes.

God is the chief Creator and Designer of all that is lovely, beautiful, and good. Since we are made in His image, we are called to create and bring beauty and goodness into existence. As little girls, our fingers often smelled of crayons and glue sticks. We would proudly present our prized artwork to family members with a big smile.

Many years later, our crayons have been replaced with smartphones and other devices. Now our innate desire to create gets overshadowed by the compulsion to consume. Targeted marketing campaigns track our likes and preferences online and place advertisements suited to our tastes right in front of our eyes. We're one click away from a shiny new purchase the internet picked out just for us. We find enough is never enough, and we always need a little bit more. We buy the lie that the more we consume, the happier, more beautiful, and more desirable we'll become.

My heart seems to sing when my doorbell rings, signaling another brown box delivery. I'm embarrassed to admit I often forget what I even ordered. I find fleeting satisfaction in my constant consumerism. As my house and closet get more cluttered, the more frustrated and anxious I become. I've discovered that the satisfaction I get from buying shiny new things is fleeting and usually disappointing.

But as we continue to over-consume, deep in our soul we have an unmet longing to create things of value and beauty. If we ignore this longing and cave in to over-consumerism, we miss out on one of our biggest purposes—the purpose to create good and meaningful things. And the world misses out on what we have to offer.

We haven't been made to create perfect things, but worthy things.

You have been intentionally designed to create in a unique way. The possibilities are endless. My friend Megan creates a loving, beautiful home for her husband and children and paints portraits and seascapes on giant canvases. My friend Kaci creates light and airy photographs of families and landscapes. My friend Jessica created an organization to fight sex trafficking of children in Hawaii. We haven't been made to create perfect things, but worthy things. We've been designed to create art, music, families, relationships, poetry, crafts, and even charitable organizations and businesses—anything that improves the lives of others or makes the world just a little bit better.

When we co-create with God by bringing forth things of value into the world, we are living a life of contribution. A life of contribution is an outward-focused life; it creates more than it takes. A life of over-consumption takes more than it gives. I believe we have been hardwired by God to contribute more than we consume.

What are the things you loved to do as a little girl? If you had a free day, how would you spend it? Ask God to show you what He is calling you to co-create with Him. Maybe you feel compelled to start a new club on your campus or create a space in your home for other women to gather. Perhaps you feel the tug to take up photography or bake desserts for foster children.

A Bible verse I love says, "Make it your ambition to lead a quiet life: You should mind your own business and work with your hands" (1 Thessalonians 4:11). The wisdom in this verse is so opposite of our culture today. I think of the strong women generations before us who homesteaded the land, lived in the present moment, and worked hard with their hands to provide for their families. In our world, it seems like everyone is living out loud so it's hard to mind our own business. With one look at your screen you can see what your favorite celebrity ate for breakfast or what your friends did without you last night.

There are three principles in this verse that could transform our lives if we put them into practice. How could your life change for the better if you led a quieter, more private life, stayed focused in your own lane, and created things? I believe if we did these three rhythms, our anxiety levels would decrease, our happiness would increase, and the world would be a more beautiful place because of what we create and contribute.

Comparison and distraction are two of the biggest killers of creativity. We look at the amazing work another woman has made and measure our work against hers. When we feel like we don't measure up or that our work is not good enough, we sometimes stop creating altogether or get down on ourselves. I think living a quieter life and minding your own business can mean shutting out what everyone else is doing (or posting online) so you can focus on your own life and passions.

If comparison doesn't kill our creativity, distraction certainly will. We have not been created to be constantly plugged in and digitally connected. We create our best work when we are focused, free from notifications and constant pings. If we are going to create deep work or beautiful and meaningful things, it is important to create space for your brain to focus and daydream without constant interruption. Ask yourself how you can live a less distracted and less digitally connected life so you can better live out your purpose to create.

One year at a young women's conference, I spoke on a panel with a talented woman named Morgan Harper Nichols who has created beautiful art with her hands and words. Morgan invites people to send her their personal stories. In response to these stories, she creates illustrated poetry and shares it online using social media as a force for good.

During the panel, Morgan said: "One of the reasons I started sharing on social media is because I had a moment with God where I felt God was saying, 'Morgan, I am the Creator and I put you here to create, not just to consume.'" Morgan went on to say, "I believe God has given every single person the ability to create something. For some of you it's art or music, and for some of you it's space at the lunch table for the girl who feels left out."[1] Morgan had a moment in her creative journey where she shifted her mindset and made her artwork about encouraging and serving others.

God is inviting us into a greater story. I believe God is calling you to a countercultural way of creating. Whether we're creating space for the girl who feels left out or making baked goods for someone who needs cheering up, we are called to create things that elevate and serve others, and in doing so, we glorify God. Whatever you are called to make, make it to the glory of God.

Take some time to reflect and dream about what it means for you to work figuratively or literally with your hands. Consider how you can stay in your own lane and show up for your life with more awe and presence. This is the season you will create things—meaningful, worthy, and beautiful things.

Be Still and Be Loved

A TIME TO REFLECT

How can you create and live a quieter life of deep presence and contentment?

God,
Thank You that You are the Creator of all that is good. Thank You that as Your image bearer, You have made me to create. Show me how to live a quieter life of deep presence and contentment. Help me stay in my own lane and fight the trap of comparison and distraction. Awaken in me a passion to create things that make this world a more beautiful place.

20

Made for Forgiveness

She finds new beginnings at the throne of grace.

*C*orrie ten Boom was a Dutch watchmaker who hid persecuted Jews in her home during World War II. Driven by her faith, Ten Boom and her family members helped many Jews escape from the Nazis. She and her entire family were caught and imprisoned in a concentration camp; her sister died, but Ten Boom, miraculously, was released.

Years later, in 1947, she came to defeated Germany to speak at a church in Munich about forgiveness. She said to the crowd, "When we confess our sins, God casts them into the deepest ocean, gone forever."[1] After she finished giving her message, she spotted a heavyset, balding man dressed in an overcoat making his way to her. She recognized him as her former prison guard. She reflected on the horrors she experienced at the hands of those guards. He couldn't have remembered her, but she could never forget him.

He approached Ten Boom, telling her, "I have become a Christian. I know that God has forgiven me for the cruel things I did there [in the concentration camp], but I would like to hear it from your lips as well . . . will you forgive me?"[2]

In that moment, Jesus' words washed over her: "If you do not forgive men their trespasses, neither will your Father forgive your trespasses" (Matthew 6:15 NKJV).

As he extended his hand out to her, Ten Boom stalled, praying silently: "Jesus, help me! I can lift up my hand. I can do that much. You supply the feeling."[3] Then she said to the man, "I forgive you. With all my heart." As they joined hands, Ten Boom later explained, "This healing warmth seemed to flood my whole being, bringing tears to my eyes."[4]

C. S. Lewis said, "Everyone says forgiveness is a lovely idea, until they have something to forgive."[5] Sometimes, someone greatly sins against us and deeply wounds us. It is natural to experience bitterness and anger. But God desires that we come to Him with our hurt and our honest emotions. He can handle our anger, disappointment, and bitterness. He will fight our battles for us so we don't need to retaliate out of pain. Forgiveness doesn't always happen overnight. For some it can be an ongoing journey that takes a long time. Be patient and believe that God will bring justice on your behalf.

The Bible repeatedly makes clear that we are called to do the hard thing and forgive like Corrie ten Boom did, just as we have been forgiven. Peter, one of Jesus' disciples, asked Him: "Lord, how often should I forgive someone who sins against me? Seven times?" "No, not seven times," Jesus replied, "but seventy times seven!" (Matthew 18:21–22 NLT).

We are to forgive because He first forgave us. We are human and regularly miss the mark. We fall short of the holiness of God by going against the way He calls us to live. But God is merciful: "But God demonstrates his own love for us in this: While we were still sin-

> **We can be empowered to extend forgiveness to those who have hurt us.**

ners, Christ died for us" (Romans 5:8). Our trespasses were also put to death and we received forgiveness and eternal life.

When we realize how God in His lovingkindness has forgiven us, we can be empowered to extend forgiveness to those who have hurt us. In circumstances such as abuse, your health and safety are a priority, and it is important that you get help. Remember, it pains God tremendously anytime we have been hurt because we are His children. God will bring justice for you: "God is just: He will pay back trouble to those who trouble you and give relief to you who are troubled, and to us as well" (2 Thessalonians 1:6–7).

Forgiveness doesn't mean you have forgotten what someone has done to you or that you need to let that person back into your life. Forgiveness is about past reconciliation, but we can choose who is worthy of being a part of our future.

Forgiveness is not forgetting or excusing your offender's behavior. Forgiveness reminds us that we are called to be instruments of peace. Jesus said, "Blessed are the peacemakers, for they will be called children of God" (Matthew 5:9). Being a peace-maker does not mean avoiding conflict or hard conversations. It is about graciously and assertively pursuing harmony in your life and relationships. "If it is possible, as far as it depends on you, live at peace with everyone" (Romans 12:18). If we are to be peacemakers, we must learn to forgive. God extends grace to us and understands that our path to forgiveness can take time. It is helpful to hear from wise and trusted voices, such as a counselor, to help you process through your pain.

We are called to not only forgive those who have hurt us, but also to love them and do good to them. Sometimes we are so hurt this seems impossible, but Jesus said, "Love your enemies, do good to those who hate you, bless those who curse you, pray for those who mistreat you" (Luke 6:27–28). When we forgive, we become free to experience greater peace and wholeness.

Sometimes we are our own worst enemy and the hardest person to forgive is ourselves. I know this from personal experience. At the age of twenty-one, when my depression became excruciating and unbearable, I tried to end my life because I was sick, deceived, and thought it was the only way I could get rid of my pain. God spared my life but as I recovered I was left with sickening feelings of guilt and shame. I had done the unthink-able and tried to end the life God had given me. Though I know God had compassion on me, I struggled with the fact that I had caused my family so much heartache and pain. I know the depression wasn't my fault, but the journey to self-forgiveness has taken time, counseling, prayer, and a deepening relationship with God.

If you have done something that calls for self-forgiveness, ask God to help you receive the love and compassion He offers you. Jesus never defines us by our mistakes. There is nothing you can do or have done that can separate you "from the love of God that is in Christ Jesus our Lord" (Romans 8:39). In Christ you are fully, completely forgiven: "He has removed our sins as far from us as the east is from the west" (Psalm 103:12 NLT). It is important that you learn from your mistakes but show yourself compassion and grace, just as God does with you.

I believe God calls us to offer forgiveness to others and ourselves because He knows it is what is best for us. Unresolved conflict, bitterness, and hurt can make us sick from the inside out, and Jesus has come to make us well. God calls us out from the past and into a brighter future. We are invited to leave our hurt, resentment, and pain before Him and trust He will fight our battles for us with justice and truth. We can move forward into the hope and future God has for us when we release the hurts, mistakes, and pain that are keeping us stuck in the past.

Are you struggling to forgive someone in your life? Is God calling you to ask someone you wronged for their forgiveness? Are you having a hard time forgiving yourself for something you have done? Don't look back, look ahead. In the book of Isaiah God says, "Forget the former things; do not dwell on the past. See, I am doing a new thing! Now it springs up; do you not perceive it? I am making a way in the wilderness and streams in the wasteland" (Isaiah 43:18–19). God wants to do a new thing in your life.

Forgiveness is a high road to take, but you will never be alone. This sometimes long, difficult road ultimately leads to wholeness and peace.

Be Still and Be Loved

A TIME TO REFLECT

What do you need to receive God's forgiveness for, and who is God calling you to forgive?

God,
Thank You that You have removed my sins as far as the east is from the west. Give me the courage and strength to offer forgiveness to those who have offended me. Examine my heart and show me where I have hurt other people. Empower me to ask for their forgiveness. Help me receive Your gift of forgiveness so I can live free.

21

Made for Sexual Wholeness

Her heart is guarded by the one true King.

We live in a sexually confused, broken world. One celebrity opened up about her sexual experiences in an interview. She disclosed that her first sexual experience was with two girls and shared that she lied to the man who later became her husband about her virginity. Before they first slept together, she told him she wasn't a virgin so "she didn't seem like a loser." She ultimately told him the truth, but their marriage ended after seven months. Regarding her sexuality, she has said, "I am literally open to every single thing" and "I don't relate to being boy or girl, and I don't have to have my partner relate to boy or girl."[1]

This approach to sexuality is becoming common and accepted. Today, our culture teaches us that our sexuality is fluid and anything goes. But is it working for us? When we survey the wreckage—STDs, pornography addiction, abortion, mental health and sexual identity issues, and the breakdown of the family—we see a generation of girls and women more broken than ever. Too many are confused about who they've been made to be and are misunderstanding the sacredness and beauty of sex as it was divinely designed. What God intended for good, Satan has perverted.

In high school, I imagined romantically losing my virginity the night of my junior prom, and by my sophomore year, many of my friends were sexually active. No one ever really talked to me about the sacredness of sex—that there was another, better way than having sex with the first guy who gave me attention. Instead, sex was no big deal. All the "cool" girls were doing it, and they wore their sexual experiences like a badge of honor.

The summer after my junior year, a friend and I traveled to my dream college for a six-week summer program. I was focused on getting straight A's in my college classes and training hard for soccer so I could make the university's team. One day after a long, humid day of training, I walked into the cafeteria and noticed a good-looking college guy staring at me. He was twenty-one and I found out he was a star football player on campus. I was taken aback when he started to give me attention. As an insecure girl, it was nice to be noticed. I thought he wanted to get to know me so I accepted when he invited me to his dorm room one night. What I hoped would innocently be the start of a dating relationship quickly became dangerous, and I was sexually assaulted.

After that experience, I felt used, dirty, and damaged—the way too many girls and women are made to feel following sexual assault, sexual harassment, and rape. Those feelings can even occur after consensual sexual encounters that are not the way God designed them to be. What he did traumatized me, and because of the shame and confusion it caused, I didn't share details about the assault for over a decade.

Our culture convinces us that having sex whenever and with whomever we want will make us worthy, powerful, and liberated. The narrative screams, "It's my body. I can do whatever I want with it." But God fashioned our bodies in the secret place and has a divine design for them. We have been intentionally created female for a set-apart purpose. For those who have surrendered their lives to Christ, our bodies are living temples where God's Spirit resides. Our body is not our own, but belongs to our holy and loving Creator.

God invites us to a better way—reserving sex for the sacred covenant of marriage between a husband and wife while calling us to lead lives of sexual integrity whether we are single, dating, or married. When we go against God's plan for sex, deep wounds eventually result. There is a divine order to our sexuality. Sex outside God's loving order can cause destruction and profound ramifications. We are free to decide how we will live and move in the bodies we have, but our choices will profoundly impact us emotionally, spiritually, and physically. Sex is not just physical. It binds two people together spiritually and emotionally, so when you break apart from someone you have been sexual with, you can, in a sense, lose a part of yourself.

The sexual trauma I experienced as a seventeen-year-old girl has been redeemed through a healthy, loving marriage where I now experience the beauty and sacredness of sex as it was created to be enjoyed. God has given clear and good boundary lines for sex that are designed to be embraced and enjoyed within the sacredness of marriage. This is for our benefit and protection from unnecessary pain.

God does not write marriage into every woman's story. Church culture often idolizes getting married and having kids, leaving those who are single or without children to feel like they are not as valuable or that God has forgotten them. This is a lie. God may have a life of singleness for you, but with Him at the center it can be a life of great purpose and satisfaction. It can be hard to be sexless and single, and it can be hard to be married. Marriage can be messy because it involves two broken people. Not every marriage ends with "happily ever after." However, when Christ is the center of a marriage and a husband and wife serve one another well, it is beautiful. Whether you are single, dating, or married, God is calling you to a life of sexual integrity or wholeness, not just physically but spiritually. He is inviting you to embrace His best for you.

If you have been bruised by your destructive sexual decisions, Jesus has come not to condemn you, but to set you free and make you whole by offering you forgiveness and inviting you to live a better way. Consider the woman in the Bible who was caught cheating on her husband and was exposed. The religious leaders dragged her in front of a crowd where she awaited her death sentence.

The Old Testament law required anyone caught in adultery to be stoned. I imagine the woman was drenched with shame, regret, and humiliation—the same way many women feel after engaging in sexual relationships outside of a healthy marriage.

This mob of prideful men came to Jesus and said, "The law of Moses says to stone her. What do you say?" (John 8:5 NLT). Jesus stooped down and wrote something with His finger in the dirt. We don't know what Jesus wrote that day in the sand, but the words He wrote were drenched in grace. That was Jesus' way.

The mob demanded an answer from Jesus. He stood up and said, "Let the one who has never sinned throw the first stone!" (John 8:7 NLT). One by one the accusers slipped away, leaving Jesus alone with the woman. He asked her, "Where are your accusers? Didn't even one of them condemn you?" "No," the woman replied. "Neither do I," Jesus said. "Go and sin no more" (John 8:10–11 NLT). Jesus offers us grace and forgiveness, freeing us from shame and inviting us into a better life.

God wants to show you who He designed you to be.

If you have been abused, raped, or assaulted, Jesus wants to love you, cleanse you, heal you, and fight for you. Psalm 147:3 says, "He heals the brokenhearted and binds up their wounds." If you are struggling with your sexuality, God wants to show you who He designed you to be and lead you to a life of great purpose. If you have made sexually destructive choices, Jesus wants to take your hand and show you a better way to live. With Jesus, it is never too late to be made new. It is never too late to choose a life of sexual integrity and experience the wholeness that comes from living the way God created us to live. Are you willing to shut out the lies our culture is telling you about sex and to trust God's best for you?

Be Still and Be Loved

A TIME TO REFLECT

What lies about your sexuality and worth are you believing, and how can you pursue sexual purity?

God,
Help me embrace Your plan for my sexuality. Give me wisdom in any romantic relationships and help me guard my heart and body. Please heal any places of sexual brokenness and show me how to establish my identity in You whether I am single, dating, or married. I trust You, God, with my heart and sexuality.

22

Made to Live Wisely

She leans not on her own understanding.

We all have one underestimated superpower that can transform our lives for the good: the power to live and choose wisely. While it is God who ultimately determines our steps even when we make our plans (Proverbs 16:9), He gives us freedom to make big and small decisions that can impact the trajectory of our lives.

We get to decide how we are going to spend the twenty-four hours we're given each day. We get to choose who we are going to be friends with, what we are going to look at on our phones, and who we date or marry if we want a relationship. We are responsible for the decisions we make every day. God stands ready to help us live with wisdom. If we lack wisdom, all we need do is ask God, who gives it to us generously (James 1:5).

The other side of wisdom is foolishness. While the Bible is full of endless wisdom for how to live our best lives, it also warns us about living foolishly. One of the verses that makes me laugh out loud is, "A beautiful woman who lacks discretion is like a gold ring in a pig's snout" (Proverbs 11:22 NLT). It might be a funny word picture, but it's sad when you watch a woman full of potential self-destruct by making poor decisions.

Throughout Scripture, and especially in the book of Proverbs, we see God contrast wisdom and foolishness. Written primarily by King Solomon, Proverbs contains short, poetic reflections on life, relationships, and the world. They are full of helpful instruction that can guide us on the path of wisdom as we go about our lives. A proverb a day can keep drama and destruction away.

Proverbs 9:10 says, "The fear of the LORD is the beginning of wisdom, and knowledge of the Holy One is understanding." The Greek word in the Bible that is translated "fear" means to revere and have holy reverence. It is our respect for God and desire to live His way that puts us in a position to live wisely and ultimately empowers us to lead better lives. The Holy Spirit is our wise Counselor empowering us to live with discretion and insight.

I believe there are three main areas of our lives for which we need wisdom:

- How we spend our time
- What relationships we choose to have
- What lifestyle choices we make

How you spend your time includes what media you consume, how much sleep you get, what you do educationally or professionally, how much time you invest in your relationship with God, and what you do with your free time.

Having wisdom in relationships means choosing as your close friends those who are seeking after God and who treat you lovingly. Wisdom means looking for red flags before you start dating someone. It means not becoming romantically involved with someone

Wisdom in lifestyle choices means pulling the weeds out of our life.

with whom you're "unequally yoked" (2 Corinthians 6:14 ESV), or someone who doesn't share your faith. It means learning how to have boundaries with toxic people and asking God to teach you how to love the people in your life well.

Wisdom in lifestyle choices means pulling the weeds out of our life (as we discussed in chapter 7, "Made to Bloom"). It's creating rhythms, habits, and routines that promote health and vitality rather than sickness and self-destruction. It's choosing to refrain from drugs and alcohol abuse and not putting yourself in dangerous or compromising situations. It's following the law, living within your financial means, and taking good care of your body.

Wisdom is one of our most valuable possessions: "For wisdom is far more valuable than rubies. Nothing you desire can compare with it" (Proverbs 8:11 NLT). Though we're not promised an easy, pain-free life, and living wisely doesn't make us immune to hardship, blessing and honor follow a woman of wisdom. God's favor is upon her: "Know also that wisdom is honey for you: If you find it, there is a future hope for you, and your hope will not be cut off" (Proverbs 24:14).

Sometimes we face a major crossroads in life. Our future can look like a blank canvas, leaving us paralyzed. Overwhelmed, we might not know what path to take. This crossroads could be deciding what college to attend, what job to take, where to move, or whether to start your own business.

I remember being twenty-three and sitting on the bed in my studio apartment, praying for wisdom in a decision to continue my relationship with my now-husband. I could see a future with him and knew we were headed toward engagement, but I wondered if I was supposed to stay single. As I prayed, a pervading sense of peace continued to come over me as I envisioned my future with him. I feel grateful that God guided me to make what turned out to be by far one of the best decisions of my life—a decision I made prayerfully and intentionally. But looking back, I believe God's blessing would still have been on my life if I decided to stay single as long as I was seeking Him.

We can bring these big decisions to God and ask Him to give us wisdom for what path to take. While big decisions such as these impact the rest of our lives, be assured that God is with you wherever you go as you seek to honor and glorify Him with your life. We must remember that even when life doesn't go the way we plan or we don't make the best decisions, we can never flee from God's presence (Psalm 139:7). He is with us everywhere we go and we are never without His help.

We are already equipped with spiritual maturity to make wise and life-giving decisions: "His divine power has given us everything we need for a godly life through our knowledge of him who called us by his own glory and goodness" (2 Peter 1:3). As

God reveals truth to us, it is ultimately our decision how we are going to respond. Are we going to be obedient and walk on the path that leads to a better life, or are we going to do life our way?

I have learned that in addition to regular Scripture reading and prayer, surrounding myself with wise women who love God has helped me make good life decisions. My mentors are always there to pray with me and offer advice and counsel. I trust them because I see fruit in their lives and know they are passionately pursuing truth and righteousness. Seek out wise mentors who can be voices of truth and encouragement to you.

In Proverbs 31, we are presented with a portrait of the "Wife of Noble Character." This passage describes a virtuous woman who loves God. Though it isn't describing an actual woman, it is painting an ideal picture of feminine wisdom. Verse 10 says, "A wife of noble character who can find? She is worth far more than rubies." Verse 26 continues, "She speaks with wisdom, and faithful instruction is on her tongue." This wise woman is rare. She is hard to find. Her value comes from her character, from the depths of who she is. This noble woman values family, works hard, is a good steward of her resources, is financially savvy, serves the needy, and glorifies God with her life.

While it seems like a tall order for us as women to follow, the noble woman in Proverbs is an example we can aspire to and she possesses qualities we can emulate. She is "clothed with strength and dignity, and she laughs without fear of the future" (Proverbs 31:5 NLT). Her character is her strongest asset. She is full of joy and doesn't live in fear because she trusts God with her future.

It is easy to live life on our own terms—to make our own choices and do as we please without looking to God. But when we live by our own desires, we face serious consequences.

Destruction eventually follows and we get hurt or cause others pain. Instead, God invites us to live in accordance with His divine order for life because He loves us and wants to protect us. God will never force us to follow His precepts or walk the narrow road. Only we can choose to become wisely women whose worth is greater than all the riches of the world. Live wisely and be a hard-to-find woman. With God's help, you have the power to choose wisely and live a better life.

Be Still and Be Loved

A TIME TO REFLECT

What area of your life do you need wisdom in?

God,
Empower me to choose wisely. Teach me to live with discretion. I want to be a wise woman who builds her house on a strong foundation. Protect me from foolishness and self-destruction as I seek to walk the narrow road that leads to life.

23

Made to Be Present

She's trading a distracted life for her actual life.

Halfway on the drive to one of our favorite surfing beaches our phones lose connection. Before we drop service, my fingers are often glued to my phone as I find various ways to keep my mind and thumb occupied. But as we reach the entrance to the windy coastal canyon framed with golden hills and expansive oak trees, I surrender my device and begin to soak in the wonder right in front of me. Gidget, who still manages to sit on my lap, sticks her head out our van's window, her pink tongue dangling in the wind. As we round that final bend, the deep blue ocean makes its appearance and I feel instantly refreshed. For a day it's just us, the salty air, and the beauty of the sea.

In a noisy and distracting world, God politely whispers, inviting us to live fully present and engaged with the life He has given us before it passes us by. It's a much-awaited invitation our souls crave to accept. The question is, will we get quiet enough to hear it? Will we show up for our life? Busyness, constant pings, and phone addiction make us strangers to our own lives. All the noise prevents us from hearing God's whisper inviting us to a better life.

Living distracted and detached from our actual life takes a toll on our happiness and mental health. I'm sure it's not news to you that much research overwhelmingly links social media use to heightened levels of anxiety and depression. Skyrocketing rates of suicide among teen girls are correlated with the onset of smartphones and social media.[1] Even with this knowledge, we keep returning to the time-sucking digital places that make us anxious and sad. I don't know a single girl or woman who has an emotionally healthy relationship with social media. I'm no exception.

As we constantly refresh our screens seeking new "likes" to things we have posted, and as we watch the filtered highlight reels of friends, celebrities, and strangers unfold before us, we experience envy and comparison and it steals our joy. Meanwhile, our own life goes neglected. These thieves rob us of contentment: "A heart at peace gives life to the body, but envy rots the bones" (Proverbs 14:30). Living immersed in the online lives of others is making us sick while keeping us from the true connection we crave.

We live in a culture where it seems everyone is producing their own *filtered* reality show on their phones, competing for attention. FOMO or "fear of missing out" on what other people are doing is real and it's what keeps us coming back for what's making us sick. We're afraid to miss out on other people's lives, but are we afraid of missing out on our own life? I believe the more we know about the daily ins and outs of other peoples' lives, the more asleep we are to our own lives. We are called to live spiritually awake: "Wake up, sleeper, rise from the dead" (Ephesians 5:14).

How do we find the path back to peace in a loud world that never slows down? How do we find a sense of value in a world where the noisiest girls online get all the attention? It's in the stillness, in the calming of our minds, that we find respite. As we shut out the distractions, we wake up to the life in front of us. As the Dutch professor and theologian Henri Nouwen said, "God is always where we are. Not in the past (with its disappointments) nor in the future (with its worries) but in the present where love can touch us."[2]

While God can use significant events to get our attention, He doesn't shout or fight to make Himself heard amidst the unnecessary chatter of our lives. God is always speaking, and it's only when we're present that we can hear Him. He is that still, small voice kindly beckoning us to be quiet in His presence so we can be filled with peace and joy.

Living in the moment means living without escaping into the past, avoiding the distractions of the present and not fearing the future. It means we are then awake to the gifts right in front of us. As my dear friend Kate Merrick says in her book *Here, Now*, "We are meant to breathe in today, and only today."[3]

You are made to live wide-awake to the story God is writing in your life. The psalmist writes, "You make known to me the path of life; you will fill me with joy in your presence, with eternal pleasures at your right hand" (Psalm 16:11). Ultimately, living in the present is an ongoing journey of abiding in God through His Spirit, moment by moment, breath by breath. To be present is to be fully engaged in the ordinary, mundane, difficult, and beautiful moments of your life.

Presence is a spiritual discipline. Living present means leaning in and investing in your dreams and desires. Presence is also sitting with uncomfortable feelings. It forces us to hear the lies we've been believing and search for the truth. It's immersing yourself in both the good and hard parts of the season you are in. It's giving the people you are with your full attention because you see their worth. It's setting boundaries with technology and even deleting those addictive apps for a while or forever. It can look like being mysterious online so you can be spiritually alive and live awake offline. It's unplugging and getting outside in creation. It's savoring a day of rest each week. It's quieting all the noise so your thoughts can wander uninterrupted. It's learning to gain strength from the practice of solitude. The path to peace is paved with presence. Presence births contentment and contentment cultivates joy. You were made for both.

While our infatuation with the lives of others might keep us from living rooted in the present, we are also sometimes consumed by the past or preoccupied with the future. Understandably, unhealed hurt, trauma, abuse, and loss can make us live in the past. On the other hand, we can spend our moments in anxiety, afraid of the future. We can also fall into the trap of thinking that our lives will finally begin at some future moment. When's the last time you thought, *Once I lose that weight, I'll be happy*, or *Once I meet that guy, I'll be happy*, or *Once I* fill-in-the-blank, *I'll be happy*? We can find ourselves ruminating on the past, anxious about what's ahead, or imagining a happier future while the present is passing us by.

Gidget is my daily teacher in the art of presence with many lessons to share. She does not multitask, dwell on the past, or worry about tomorrow. When she eats, she does so with focus and gusto. When it's time for a good scratch, she lies on her back, kicks her four paws to the sky, and wiggles hysterically. And when it's time to play, she gets the "zoomies," running circles in our backyard with a smile on her face.

God is inviting you to breathe in life one day at a time. He is hoping you will wake up to the life He's given you before it passes you by. He promises to be your provider, giving you everything you need for each moment. God will safekeep you or "hem [you] in behind and before" (Psalm 139:5), enveloping you with love and protection. He will heal your past hurts and fight your battles. You are invited to be transformed by His Spirit moment by moment as you live present and wide awake to the story He is writing for you right here, right now.

Be Still and Be Loved

A TIME TO REFLECT

What are some tangible things you can do to help you practice the spiritual discipline of presence?

God,
Give me the courage to lean into my actual life. Help me wake up before it passes me by. Teach me what it means to be present. Give me the wisdom to know what's distracting me from the fullness of the present and the courage to cut these things out of my life. Heal me of my past hurts and give me peace for the future so I can live wide awake.

24

Made to Rest

She's finding peace that restores her soul.

I walk through the big blue door of my friend Leyla's ranch house and am greeted with the delicious scent of freshly baked challah bread. Paul and I receive bear hugs from Leyla, her husband, and two children. It's Friday in the Santa Ynez Valley and the sun has just set, painting the mountains behind their home with a purple hue. We leave our phones and distractions behind and welcome Shabbat, the biblical Sabbath or holy day of rest. We expectantly embrace this set-apart evening of food, friendship, and blessing. There is no work or distraction. Instead, we are fully present with one another and at peace.

Leyla is Jewish and had a life-changing encounter with Yeshua (Jesus) at the age of fourteen. She has been following Him

155

ever since. She regularly practices the biblical rhythms, including Shabbat and the many Jewish celebrations. Every Friday, minutes before sunset, she lights two candles, signaling the beginning of the sacred day, and recites a blessing. She and her family set all work and distractions aside. Together they eat a festive meal and bless one another with prayers. Their sacred day of rest continues until the first three stars appear in the sky on Saturday. It always feels so special to celebrate Shabbat with Leyla and her family. The experience challenges me and reminds me to take a break from my work and striving and to honor God by observing a holy day of rest each week.

Sabbath, which means "to rest," is a foundational part of God's original design for the world. Through this holy ancient rhythm, we see that God works and God rests, and we are called to do the same: "So the creation of the heavens and the earth and everything in them was completed. On the seventh day God had finished his work of creation, so he rested from all his work. And God blessed the seventh day and declared it holy, because it was the day when he rested from all his work of creation" (Genesis 2:1–3 NLT). This is the first use of the word "holy" in Scripture, where the seventh day is declared as the only blessed day of the week.

Honoring the Sabbath is also the fourth of the ten commandments: "Remember the Sabbath day by keeping it holy. Six days you shall labor and do all your work, but the seventh day is a sabbath to the LORD your God. On it you shall not do any work" (Exodus 20:8–10).

When is the last time you took twenty-four hours off work or away from noise and distraction to share a meal, bless others, relax, daydream, thank God, and do the things you love and enjoy? Sadly, many of us see the seventh day of our week as another chance to get ahead.

Throughout Scripture, God has repeatedly made clear how important the Sabbath is to Him. God is worthy of our worship and knows our souls are hungry for rest. We have been created to be still and to be restored by regularly embracing rhythms of rest and renewal.

If we attend church, we might see that as our weekly holy ritual. Something we can check off our list of things to do. But once our church service concludes, we often go back to our work and worries.

God does not measure our worth by our output.

God is inviting us into something better. He wants to restore our souls. God wants us to trust that He is our provider and that we can take a day off and entrust it to Him. Honoring the Sabbath is an opportunity to trust that God will provide for us and that our work will be accomplished even as we rest.

The Sabbath reminds us that God does not measure our worth by our output. He doesn't love us because of what we do, how hard we hustle, or how much we succeed. The gospel assures us that we are fully loved just as we are, apart from anything we have to offer. The world will go on without our efforts.

Sometimes religious words like the Sabbath may sound obscure and uninviting. They might sound boring and constrictive. However, having a day of rest each week restores us and invites us to reflect on our lives. It helps us live our best lives and become women who experience wholeness and freedom as well as better mental health.

For followers of Christ, the Sabbath is not designed to be a day of rigid rules or restrictions, but a day of freedom. It is not about legalism, but about our hearts. Jesus said, "The Sabbath was made for man, not man for the Sabbath" (Mark 2:27). Jewish culture had made Sabbath a burden and almost intolerable with so many restrictions. Here Jesus makes clear that a holy day of rest is for our physical, mental, and spiritual benefit. It is a divine gift that restores our souls. God's boundaries for us are always rooted in love, but sometimes we wrongly interpret this love as a sense of religious obligation.

While Christians have traditionally observed their day of rest on Sundays, I don't believe the actual day of your Sabbath matters so much as long as you make a commitment to be still and restored one day a week. Having a sacred day of rest gives you a dedicated time to celebrate God and what He has done for you. It gives you the opportunity to trust that even in times of stress and hustle, you can believe that God will go before you to move mountains in your life so you can find rest and renewal in Him.

Rest is a pillar of good mental health. It invites you to experience a reprieve from not only the stress of your own life, but also from the noise of watching everyone else's lives unfold through social media. Consider putting your phone away on your day of rest so you can invest in relationships in person and enjoy your actual life. Sabbath is an opportunity to tend to the garden of your life with worship, community, and play.

Research on rest has found that it reduces stress, restores mental energy, increases creativity, improves short term memory, boosts productivity, and even adds years to your life.[1] There are many gifts waiting for us when we prioritize times of rest in our lives. The rhythm of rest does not need to be reserved only for your Sabbath day. We can incorporate life-giving times of rest into our daily lives. We can tuck our phone into bed hours before we go to sleep, and not check our email or work when we're off the clock. As part of your soul care you can incorporate into your day restorative activities that you enjoy, like long walks, listening to music, or taking baths.

Dream up your perfect day of rest, worship, and play. What are the activities that restore your soul? When do you feel most alive? When do you feel closest to God? What in your life is draining you and causing you stress and anxiety? Take a day each week to remove yourself from those things as you experience restoration and peace. Go for a hike. Jump in a lake or the ocean. Share a meal with family or friends. Journal. Take a nap. This weekly rhythm of rest will help you thrive and plant deep roots so you can bloom even more beautifully. Ultimately, a day of rest is a gift God has given us to remember Him and to help us flourish. Are you ready to receive it?

Be Still and Be Loved

A TIME TO REFLECT

What are some practical ways you can incorporate rhythms of rest and renewal into both your daily life and one set-apart day a week?

God,
Thank You that You are sovereign in my life and that I can trust You to direct my life even while I rest. Thank You for the gift of rest, and teach me what it means to make this a weekly rhythm of my life.

25

Made for an Outward-Focused Life

In her presence, you are loved and known.

*I*n high school I was imprisoned by social anxiety and insecurity. At the grocery store checkout line, I couldn't look
the clerk in the eye, and my hand would shake when signing the
receipt. In conversation with acquaintances or people I didn't
know well, instead of listening, I was more concerned with how
I was composing myself and with what I should say next. My face
frequently turned red any time I was nervous or around someone
I wanted to impress.

In the nineteenth century writer Stendhal's novel *Le Rouge et le Noir* (*The Red and the Black*), there is a narcissistic character named Mathilde. The character Prince Korasoff says about her, "She looks at herself instead of looking at you, and so doesn't know you."[1] I spent so many years looking at myself that, like Mathilde, I didn't see the people in my life the way I should have. Whether it was clinical depression or normal teenage insecurity or a combination of both, I was consumed by myself. My thoughts were usually turned inward and I was plagued by a sense of inferiority that made me a prisoner in my own life.

On my nightstand stood my stack of teen magazines and self-help books and my journal where I recorded my deepest, inmost thoughts. The messages I heard in these pages convinced me I just needed to love myself, but the problem was I didn't like myself. I didn't know how to love someone I didn't even like. Our world promises that self-love will cure our sense of insecurity. *You are enough! Love your flaws! Just love yourself!*

> **Our world promises that self-love will cure our sense of insecurity. . . . But what we really need is a love greater than the love of self.**

But what we really need is a love greater than the love of self. We need the Author of love to heal us and make us whole from the inside out.

We are flawed and fall short of the glory of God (Romans 3:23). Apart from God we are not enough. We are not okay, and when we live detached from the supernatural love and forgiveness God freely gives, we will never fully be at peace with ourselves or love the skin that we're in. Our own self-love apart from the love of God will fall short. It will never be enough. The love of Christ rescues us from ourselves. He offers His love unconditionally and eternally, and it finds us in our shortcomings and inadequacies.

Jesus tells us in what is called the Great Commandment, "Love the Lord your God with all your heart and with all your soul and with all your strength and with all your mind"; and "Love your neighbor as yourself" (Luke 10:27). God invites us to have a healthy love of ourselves, and He calls us to love Himself and others well. When Jesus says, "love your neighbor as yourself," He presupposes that we already have love for ourselves. This does not mean that we all love ourselves the way God desires us to or that we don't struggle with low self-esteem. Instead, I think Jesus was alluding to the reality that most of us put our own needs before others. We think of ourselves before we think of our neighbors. This innate self-focus can sometimes manifest in pride or insecurity, or both.

When I try to soothe my insecurity by trying to fix myself and become the woman I think I should be, the more self-consumed I become and the more I struggle. However, the more I rest in my intrinsic worth in Christ, the more freedom I experience. The more I forget myself and relax into God's love for me, the more wide-awake I am to the people and experiences around me.

There were seasons where I was so sick I was unable to look beyond myself. I know God had compassion on me. But as I got help for my mental health and I began to receive God's love, I also began to learn how to love others better, and doing so brought me healing and purpose. I am still learning to stop trying to fix myself and just let God love me.

God is inviting you to do the same.

It is often said, "Humility isn't thinking less of yourself, it's thinking of yourself less."[2] Thinking of yourself less frees you to think of others more. To be "free of me" is to be free indeed. In his book *The Freedom of Self-Forgetfulness*, pastor Tim Keller writes, "The truly gospel-humble person is a self-forgetful person whose ego is just like his or her toes. It just works. It does not draw attention to itself. The toes just work; the ego just works. Neither draws attention to itself."[3]

I've discovered the more I take a genuine interest in other people, the more secure I am with who I am. One beauty secret is this: you will become more beautiful in one day by loving other people than you will in one year by trying to get other people to love you. What we notice about women who know their God-given worth is that they are genuinely interested in others. They are not striving to be seen or hustling to be heard. They are at ease. They know that in Christ they are enough. In their presence we feel loved and seen. A woman who knows her value is not self-loathing or overly self-loving. She is secure, at peace, and clothed in humility and kindness. She is the kind of woman whose company we want to keep. The thing we remember about being in her presence is how she makes us feel.

We each wear an invisible sign that says, "Make me feel valued." One of the reasons we exist is to make each other feel significant and to display God's love to one another. God gave us each other to extinguish our loneliness and unworthiness with His divine love—a love that is most fully expressed in listening to, encouraging, and serving one another. Be the woman who sees this sign on the people she meets and affirms them through words and actions. The world is starving for kind women who look beyond themselves.

Our culture is lying to us, making us believe self-exaltation is the path to love and success. The world has plenty of women who are lovers of themselves. Our world needs secure, set-apart women who know their true value and purpose, empowering them to be lovers of God and humanity. Our world is desperate for women who live wide awake to the needs of a lonely, dispirited world and are ready to be the helpers, the encouragers, and the listeners.

As you turn to God for your identity and worth, He will begin to heal and empower you to turn your eyes outward. He will stir in you a desire to go and serve the people in front of you. When we are secure in God's love, it overflows to those around us. The more we turn our gaze from our own reflection, the more alive we become. Look up and be the woman whose presence makes others feel loved and known.

Be Still and Be Loved

A TIME TO REFLECT

How can you make the people in your life feel valued?

Lord,
I confess that I often look inward more than outward. Please heal the insecure and prideful parts of me with Your supernatural love. Fill me up so I can overflow with love. Heal me as I look to You for my true worth. Empower me to love others well and make them feel seen, known, and loved the way I feel in Your presence.

26

Made for a Mission

She tells the world of the love that rescued her.

After a four-hour canoe ride upstream followed by a three-hour hike, we reached our destination—a tiny straw hut hidden in the jungles of Panama, Central America. We met a family of seven, part of the native Emberá tribe. Our team of college students had traveled from Southern California to help them with various projects, including building a latrine. Our trip also included visiting orphanages and doing street ministry in the country. That night, our team and host family spoke in broken Spanish and shared bowls of rice with yuccas. The next morning, our leader asked me to join Minella, a thirteen-year-old girl from the tribe, on a trip to get more yuccas for that night's dinner. She handed me some coins, and I tucked them into the pockets of my khaki pants.

"¿Cuántos años tiene?" (How old are you?), I asked Minella.

"Trece," she said.

I continued asking Minella any question I could think of until I exhausted my Spanish vocabulary.

"¿Hay cocodrilos aquí?" (Are there crocodiles here?), I asked.

"Sí, sí," she said, smiling as I screamed in fear, water up to my waist.

We trekked slowly up the river. A sudden mist fell from the sky. As we made our way around the bend, my jaw dropped. Thousands of delicate, lavender-colored flowers floated downstream. The water was up to our waist and the mist turned into a heavy rainfall. With my index finger, I began picking up the tiny lavender flowers, placing them on Minella's hair one after another.

She beamed. Following my lead, she lifted a flower on the tip of her finger and placed it on the crown of my head. We continued taking turns putting flowers in one another's hair until dozens of flowers covered our heads.

"God loves you, Minella," I said, placing one last flower in her hair.

She smiled radiantly.

To be used by God is the greatest adventure. We have been made for a mission. That mission is to tell others the good news that God loves them and has sent His Son Jesus into this broken world to rescue us, forgive our sins, and give us the gift of eternal life. The word "mission" means "sending." Jesus said, "As the Father has sent me, I am sending you" (John 20:21).

The mission of believers to share the good news is referred to as the Great Commission. Eleven of Jesus' disciples traveled to a mountain in Galilee. Then Jesus came to them and said:

"All authority in heaven and on earth has been given to me. Therefore go and make disciples of all nations, baptizing them in the name of the Father and of the Son and of the Holy Spirit, and teaching them to obey everything I have commanded you. And surely I am with you always, to the very end of the age." (Matthew 28:18–20)

Before we can be sent, we need to know what it really means to be a disciple. The word "Christian" is used in the Bible only three times. Before Jesus' followers were called Christians, they were referred to as disciples. A disciple is a believer in and follower of Jesus—one who closely follows His way of loving and living and who obeys and practices His teachings. Just as Jesus sent out His disciples to spread His message, we have also been called to "go" and invite others to follow Him and be transformed by His love.

While collectively the church is called to reach people across the globe, we do not need to cross oceans or continents to fulfill this holy mission. We are sent into our families, communities, and daily spheres of influence to share what God has done in our lives and to tell of the hope He offers everyone who puts their faith in Him.

Fulfilling our mission is not comfortable or easy. It is not culturally popular or acceptable to talk about religion or to ask others what they believe about God. But we are not made for a comfortable faith. We live in a changing culture that now generally disregards God or has misunderstood Him. God is often misunderstood because He has been misrepresented. We are invited to be God's true ambassadors (2 Corinthians 5:20) and bring hope to a hurting world, clearly communicating the gospel or "good news."

Jesus said, "By their fruit you will recognize them" (Matthew 7:16). Every day we preach a sermon through the lives we lead. We don't have to be perfect to be used by God or to be sent by Him. Just look at the twelve disciples. They fought over which disciple was the greatest. Simon Peter denied even knowing Jesus three times. Judas betrayed Jesus. Thomas doubted. Like the disciples, we have our shortcomings. However, if the fruit of the Spirit—such as love, joy, gentleness, and kindness—are not evident in your life, do some self-examination and ask God to transform you so you can more effectively represent Him.

As followers of Jesus, we carry the ultimate hope people are seeking, including the answers to existential questions like "why am I here?" and "what happens when I die?" We are called to be ready to lovingly share the grace of Jesus that has rescued us: "Always be prepared to give an answer to everyone who asks you to give the reason for the hope that you have. But do this with gentleness and respect" (1 Peter 3:15). We are to be ready and equipped to give clear answers for what we believe and to do so with love and kindness.

One of the most powerful ways we can tell others about God is by sharing our testimony or the story of how we came to faith in Christ. As the psalmist said, "Come and hear, all you who fear God; let me tell you what he has done for me" (Psalm 66:16). I am always moved by the endless stories of lives that have been transformed by God. I am convinced God can transform any life, no matter how broken it may be. God can do beautiful things with a broken life.

During my struggle with severe depression, I read *Honestly* by Sheila Walsh, an author and speaker who opened up about her own battle with depression. Her story helped me understand the gospel and made me feel less alone as I wrestled with believing in God but struggling with my mental health. I have since had the privilege of sharing my own testimony in private conversation, as well as publicly before audiences of girls and women. God might not call you to speak in front of a crowd or write a book, but your testimony is equally valuable and can bring someone who is wandering home to the heart of God.

You are invited to live loved, rescued, and redeemed by Christ, and to live your life in a way that tells others of this love through your actions and words. We are called to "act justly and to love mercy and to walk humbly" with God (Micah 6:8). Are you ready to bravely go and tell others what God has done for you and what He can do for them? You are made for a mission of sharing God's love.

Be Still and Be Loved

A TIME TO REFLECT

Who has God placed in your life that you feel called to share God's love with?

God,
I want to be used by You. Help me be ready
to give an answer for the hope that is in me.
Equip me to share the story of what You have
done in my life. Open doors for me to share
Your truth and hope with those You bring into
my life. Make me brave, make me kind, and
make me a messenger of Your love and truth.

27

Made to Be Faithful

She's trustworthy with the days entrusted to her.

My grandmother Marian lived a simple, resilient life. She was born into a poor family and raised in a blue-collar Midwestern town where she lived her entire life. She met my grandfather at a youth church event, and they were married in 1941 when she was twenty-one. A few months later, Pearl Harbor was bombed and the US was at war. Part of the Greatest Generation, my grandmother endured the Great Depression and World War II, in which my grandfather fought. For over two years while he served in the Pacific, she prayed for his safety. She spent her time socializing with other "war widows," and once had to console her best friend when Army officers arrived to inform her that her husband had been killed in Italy.

When my dad was a boy, his family never once went out to dinner or took a family vacation. While lacking in wealth and material possessions, my grandma overflowed with love. Her family was her whole world. She delighted in being both a faithful wife and a mom to my dad and his older brother. Her days were filled with cooking, cleaning, hanging clothes on the line, church activities, and showering her family in hugs and kisses. Her contagious joy made everyone in her presence feel loved.

For women today, the world's portrait of success doesn't look like a simple, hard-working life. It looks like having a massive influence through a big social media following and a walk-in closet full of designer clothes. It might look like juggling your dream job with the perfect marriage and perfect kids in a perfectly decorated house. And don't forget the perfect body.

Many women are hustling themselves sick. They're chasing an ideal of success they're not even certain they want. They are hard-pressed with unrealistic and contradicting societal and cultural expectations. We are expected to be strong, yet feminine and sexual; highly successful, yet balanced and in control; charismatic and captivating, yet humble and authentic. Our culture demands us to be all these things effortlessly without room for slip-ups. We have been misled to believe that to have a full life and get every drop it has to offer, we must live out loud and do big things.

When I look back on my life as a senior in high school, I know this unrealistic standard of success was one of the factors that made me depressed. From the time I was a young girl a snowball of unrealistic standards had been forming in my mind.

These culturally influenced but self-inflicted expectations told me that living a life the world would call small or insignificant was unacceptable. I learned to hustle for my self-worth until I fell apart and discovered the true source of my worth through a relationship with Christ. I didn't understand then that God wasn't calling me to be perfect or even to do big things. He was simply inviting me to live loved and be faithful with what was right in front of me.

This material-focused standard of success can steal our joy and rob us of our true God-given purpose. It can keep us from living authentically. Instead of asking us to chase the world's definition of success, God invites us to live a faithful life. He asks us to be a good steward with everything He's given us and to live into the unique callings He's placed on our lives. In the world's eyes, some of our callings may seem simple and ordinary. They might not be flashy by the world's standards and might not generate many social media followers. But God has written a unique story for your life that is just as valuable as the life of the girl who gets all the praise and attention.

God doesn't require perfection. He doesn't demand big things from you. But He treasures faithfulness. Sometimes being faithful means working as a barista to help pay your student loan. Sometimes it means caring for your elderly grandparents or being a role model for a sibling. It's being honest and hard-working. It can mean doing the dishes, cleaning your apartment, or spending less money so you can donate some to a charity.

Faithfulness looks like rising each morning with expectation and gratitude and loving every person in your path. It's passionately pursuing your dreams and doing the hard work when no one is looking. God has given you unique gifts, desires, and relationships and invites you to be faithful with all you've been given.

In the parable of the talents in Matthew 25:14–30, Jesus tells the story of a master who left his house to travel and entrusted his property to three of his servants. To one servant he gave five bags of gold, to another two, and to another just one. He gave these bags to them according to their unique ability. The master then left. The first servant who received five bags invested them wisely and made five more. The second servant who received two made two more. The third servant who received one bag hid the money his master had given him.

When the master returned from his journey, he went to his three servants to learn what they had each done with the money he had given them. He was pleased when the first servant shared that he had made five more bags of gold. The master said to him, "Well done, good and faithful servant! You have been faithful with a few things; I will put you in charge of many things" (Matthew 25:21). The master responded the same way to the servant who had doubled his money. The third servant who hid his master's money said, "Master, I knew that you are a hard man. . . . So I was afraid and went out and hid your gold in the ground. See, here is what belongs to you" (vv. 24–25). The master was angry, calling him a "lazy servant" (v. 26). The master had him give his bag to the one who had ten and threw the servant into the darkness.

> **When it is my turn to stand before God, I don't want to be found fancy. I want to be found faithful.**

I believe God grants grace, but also that He judges justly. When our days on earth are over, we will each give an account for how we lived our lives. Some of us are called to fancier lives than others. Some of us are called to simpler, quieter, but equally meaningful lives. Stop and look at what's in front of you. Take account of your relationships, your assets, your talents, opportunities, and dreams. What does it look like for you to steward them with responsibility and faithfulness?

One of my grandmother's requests for a hymn to be played at her funeral was "How Great Thou Art." As the music director led our family and her friends in that beloved hymn, I reflected on my grandmother's life, a life perhaps ordinary in an earthly sense yet extraordinary in a heavenly sense. My heart rests assured that when she saw Jesus, He embraced her and said, "Well done, my good and faithful servant." When I get to the end of my life, and it is my turn to stand before God, I don't want to be found fancy. I want to be found faithful.

Be Still and Be Loved

A TIME TO REFLECT

What does it mean to you to live a faithful life?

Lord,
Thank You that you don't put unrealistic de-
mands on me. Thank You that You hold me to
grace, not perfection. Teach me what it looks
like to be faithful in my life with the little and
big things. Help me to steward everything
You've given me in a way that honors You.

28

Made to Be Transformed

She sets her mind on what is true.

I was eighteen and barely hanging on after depression had come like a wrecking ball, totally destroying my life as I knew it. I inhaled deep, long breaths as I tried to rub off the feeling that someone or something was about to push me off a fifty-foot ledge. My mom had recently given me a copy of Norman Vincent Peale's famous book *The Power of Positive Thinking.* I sat on my bedroom floor and opened to the first chapter. The Bible verse Philippians 4:13 NLT was written in italics:

I can do everything through Christ, who gives me strength.

With deep breaths, I repeated the first sentence over and over, hoping it would give me the strength I needed to make it through one more day.

I said it again and again but nothing happened. Nothing changed. The heaviness remained and the sadness stayed. The lies remained loud. My mind was ruminating on thoughts of self-hate—all telling me what a horrible person I was.

You're such a mess.

You don't deserve to go to college.

You need to get lost.

I was fighting a battle in my mind and I was losing. To help me regain control over my mind, I began meeting with a therapist as part of my treatment for depression. Each visit I sat on her sticky maroon leather sofa as she tried to help me identify and untwist the distorted, untrue thoughts swirling in my mind. She specialized in CBT, or Cognitive Behavioral Therapy, a form of therapy that "helps the client discover, challenge, and modify or replace their negative, irrational thoughts."[1]

We are women daily fighting a battle in our minds. Sometimes this war is caused by a broken brain that is not functioning properly and medical treatment is needed, as was true in my case. Sometimes the internal war in our head is caused by our own untrue thoughts, and other times our mind is flooded with faulty beliefs that come directly from Satan, that spiritual enemy the Bible calls the father of lies (John 8:44)." Often, the wreckage in our minds is caused by a combination of physical, chemical, and spiritual forces at play.

> **We must be like a gatekeeper on the trailways of our mind, holding every thought captive and deciding whether it can stay or must go.**

Our heart is the wellspring of life (Proverbs 4:23), but our mind determines the quality of our life. We often pray for safety as we travel and go about our day, but we rarely pray for protection and oversight over our mind. The thoughts we think determine our beliefs, attitudes, and behavior. Just as we are told to guard our heart, we must be like a gatekeeper on the trailways of our mind, holding every thought captive and deciding whether it can stay or must go.

God invites us to lead lives set apart from the world and to be changed for the better by the way we think: "Do not conform to the pattern of this world, but be transformed by the renewing of your mind" (Romans 12:2). Our mind is the hub of our spiritual transformation. We are made to be transformed into the likeness and character of Christ.

The principles behind positive thinking like those laid out in Peale's book and by CBT are not new. They have been in the Bible for thousands of years: "Finally, brothers and sisters, whatever is true, whatever is noble, whatever is right, whatever is pure, whatever is lovely, whatever is admirable—if anything is excellent or praiseworthy—think about such things" (Philippians 4:8).

If we are to be transformed, we must learn to train our minds to think in accordance with what is good and true. While not centered around God, positive thinking and pop psychology might ease the effects of negative thinking, but renewing our mind with the Word of God is what transforms us from the inside out.

This transformation or metamorphosis is a journey of taking off our former self separated from God and putting on our new identity in Christ as His chosen, loved, and redeemed child: "You were taught, with regard to your former way of life, to put off your old self, which is being corrupted by its deceitful desires; to be made new in the attitude of your minds; and to put on the new self, created to be like God in true righteousness and holiness" (Ephesians 4:22–24).

A necessary step to be made new is to cultivate an awareness of the thoughts that occupy our mind. This is not an easy task and takes time, attention, and discipline. Some people who struggle with self-defeating thoughts wear a rubber band on their wrist, which they snap anytime they recognize an untrue thought. After they catch the thought, they then observe it and replace it with one that is true.

We can ask God for the wisdom to discern lies from what is true: "If any of you lacks wisdom, you should ask God, who gives generously to all without finding fault, and it will be given to you" (James 1:5). As you ask God for insight, He will faithfully help you unveil the lies you are believing so you can replace them with His truth.

To be transformed, we must become devoted students of what is true. This means spending time in prayer and regularly reading the Bible. The psalmist gives us an example to follow: "I have hidden your word in my heart that I might not sin against you" (Psalm 119:11). Memorizing Scripture or hiding God's Word in your heart can equip you with truth in times of doubt, fear, anxiety, and uncertainty. It is our weapon for a very real spiritual battle.

I daily use memory verses and biblical truth declarations that remind me of my identity in Christ to fight lies, anxiety, and fear. I have a list of ten truths taped to my bathroom mirror that remind me of who I am, and most importantly who God is. These include "God is my refuge and strength," "I am a child of God," and "My value comes from God alone." I repeat these truths throughout my day and especially when I am struggling mentally.

Renewing our mind is a spiritual practice that has a physical effect on our brain. Repeating thoughts over and over actually creates new pathways in our brain. Neuroplasticity is the ability of the brain to form new connections and pathways and change how its circuits are wired.[2] God can physically transform and rewire our brain as we think and meditate on what is true, making it healthier and more resilient.

As we are transformed by the renewing of our minds, we lose our appetite for the things this world delights in. We become turned off by lame movies. We no longer take God's name in vain. Partying loses its appeal. Our old self fades into the past as we awaken to a new way of being that brings peace, joy, and purpose to our days.

God wants to help you fight the lies you are believing about yourself and your future. By receiving professional help when needed, and by renewing your mind with Scripture, you can go from being a woman at war with yourself to a woman at peace with yourself because Christ dwells within you. You can push back the darkness in your mind with gratitude and thanksgiving.

It is not by our own doing that we are transformed and made new. It is the power of God's Spirit at work deep within us that heals, restores, sets us free, and makes us new. God loves us as we are but invites us to be transformed into His likeness. We are made to be women who walk in the truth of who God is and who we are in Him.

Be Still and Be Loved

A TIME TO REFLECT

What are you believing about God, yourself, and your future that is untrue, and how can you renew your mind with truth?

God,
Give me the wisdom to identify the untrue thoughts and beliefs that occupy my mind. Heal my brain if it is not working the way You designed it to. Teach me how to meditate on Your word so I can be transformed from the inside out by the renewing of my mind. Make my mind strong and resilient and help me push back the darkness with gratitude and thanksgiving.

29

Made to Worship

She leaves the world more in awe of God.

One of my most prized possessions is our blue 1973 half-cab Ford Bronco I affectionately named Billie. She's the cutest little truck in our whole valley—in my humble opinion, of course. With no radio to distract me and the wind through the open window catching my long brown hair, my busy mind wanders. A few times I have envisioned Billie rusting away in a junkyard one day, as I am reminded that here on earth even the things we love the most won't last.

We spend our lives pursuing what we most value and treasure in life. The things we hold dearest keep our attention, whether it's our faith, our image, our relationships, or our achievements. We often chase our idea of the perfect life, thinking status, fame, and beauty will soothe the emptiness we run from. We live in a culture that worships stuff rather than the Giver of every good and perfect gift.

While it's okay to enjoy things and the many gifts in our lives, Jesus tenderly warns us:

> "Don't store up treasures here on earth, where moths eat them and rust destroys them, and where thieves break in and steal. Store your treasures in heaven, where moths and rust cannot destroy, and thieves do not break in and steal. Wherever your treasure is, there the desires of your heart will also be." (Matthew 6:19–21 NLT)

This truth hit home on a hot, gusty summer day when a raging California wildfire threatened our home. I was forced to pack up only a trunkful of our most needed and treasured belongings. Only a change of clothes, our photographs, computer, and a few sentimental possessions made the cut. It was a terrifying, but surprisingly liberating, experience. Earthly possessions and pursuits crumble but the things that last forever are our true treasures.

We are not made to worship things; we are made to find purpose and joy as we worship God. When we think of worship, we usually think of singing songs on Sunday morning at church or playing our favorite Christian music throughout the week. Lifting our voice in praise is one of many expressions of worship, but does not encapsulate the depth of what worship really is.

True worship, as Pastor John Piper explains, "is essentially an inner stirring of the heart to treasure God above all the treasures of the world."[1] It is also defined as "an *act* of ascribing ultimate value to something in a way that energizes and engages your whole person, your whole being."[2] We don't worship out of obligation but out of love because "he first loved us" (1 John 4:19).

The word "worship" is derived from the old English word "worthship."[3] We worship God because He has infinite worth. The root of the word "ship" means "shape." We are shaped by the things we assign worth to. What in your life are you ascribing ultimate value to that will not last?

We are wired for worship. Even those who claim they don't have a personal faith engage in worship. Countless people bow down and worship nature instead of God the Creator. Misplaced worship hap-

> **We are shaped by the things we assign worth to.**

pens not only in the great outdoors, but in sports arenas, Hollywood, clothing stores, and on social media.

In Psalm 95, we receive a model for true worship:

Come, let us sing to the LORD!
    Let us shout joyfully to the Rock of our salvation.
Let us come to him with thanksgiving.
    Let us sing psalms of praise to him. (Psalm 95:1–2 NLT)

The psalmist goes on to distinguish God above all others, "For the LORD is a great God, a great King above all gods" (v. 3 NLT). He continues, "Come, let us worship and bow down. Let us kneel before the LORD our maker, for he is our God" (v. 6 NLT).

Jesus said, "God is spirit, and his worshipers must worship in the Spirit and in truth" (John 4:24). To worship in spirit means that it is genuine and heartfelt. Referring to the Pharisees, a legalistic group of Jewish leaders, Jesus recited a prophecy from Isaiah, saying, "These people honor me with their lips, but their hearts are far from me" (Matthew 15:8). Jesus wants a relationship with us. He knows our hearts. Worship flows from a grateful heart that recognizes what Jesus has done for you. The Holy Spirit awakens our souls to the magnificence of Christ, empowering us to worship with our whole self.

To worship in truth requires that we have a right view and knowledge of God. We must understand who God really is as laid out for us in Scripture. It would be foolish and futile to worship a god of our own making based on how we think he should be, rather than looking to Jesus who is the exact representation of God (Hebrews 1:3). It is a heart knowledge of God, not just a head knowledge, that ushers us into worship. When our life has been transformed by Jesus, our natural response is to love and be devoted to Him with a grateful heart.

There are many expressions of worship, including prayer, study, singing hymns and spiritual songs, Scripture meditation, tithing, honoring the Sabbath, and fellowship. Worship doesn't begin and end on Sunday mornings. Music simply facilitates worship. To experience the fullness of joy, we must learn to dwell in God and make our home in Him.

When our faith becomes real, we are changed and there is spiritual fruit. True worship influences our behaviors and actions. Jesus said, "So you see, faith by itself isn't enough. Unless it produces good deeds, it is dead and useless" (James 2:17 NLT). Worship leads us to serve, compelling us to be used for good.

Worship is a response to who God is. It is a consuming expression of gratitude that He has come to rescue us. True worship compels us to respond with our whole being—our heart, body, mind, and spirit. But worship doesn't mean spending your life in a monk-like trance. Nor does it mean leading a life of rigid rules. Worship that is pure is filled with beauty and results in joy and peace.

Ultimately, worship is about surrender. God calls surrendered women to do incredible things. A surrendered life can look like adventure and risk, beauty and purpose. It's being the women we've been made to be: alive in God with our unique talents and gifts. Living surrendered means letting go of the earthly things we think are worthy of our utmost affection and choosing the better way. Surrender is about offering ourselves completely to God. "So use your whole body as an instrument to do what is right for the glory of God" (Romans 6:13 NLT).

My favorite song is "A Living Prayer," sung by Allison Kraus, a famous bluegrass-country singer with an angelic voice. We can make our lives a living prayer, abiding in God moment by moment as we treasure Him above all things and live with gratitude.

I want my life to be a constant prayer before God. Not because I want to be super holy or religious. I long to be a living prayer because I know when I worship God I am most alive. Joy flows from my spirit and I feel whole and free. I want to be a living prayer because Jesus has rescued me from the pit and restored me. I know that apart from Him I am nothing. God deserves nothing less for all He has done for me.

As you get to know God, you'll want to give more of yourself to Him. And as you give yourself, you will wake up to the woman you've been created to be, and the things of this world will lose their appeal. As the great hymn "Turn Your Eyes Upon Jesus" goes:

Turn your eyes upon Jesus,
Look full in His wonderful face,
And the things of earth will grow strangely dim,
In the light of His glory and grace.[4]

As you look to Christ, the value you placed on the things of this world will fade away. True worship is choosing to live surrendered—giving yourself completely to God and building your life on Him. He is the rock that will not move. You were created to worship and in worshiping you will come alive.

Be Still and Be Loved

A TIME TO REFLECT

What would it look like to live fully surrendered to God?

God,
Help me identify the people and things that I have placed too much worth in. Make me a worshiper of You and teach me to live fully surrendered before You.

30

Made to Live Fully Alive

She lives loved.

Two weeks into my second stay at a hospital psychiatric ward when I was eighteen, I was slowly beginning to come out of the dark places my mind had taken me. The feeling of no longer wanting to live was beginning to fade. As a reminder of broken dreams, I wore the sweatshirt for the college I had just withdrawn from due to my depression and a pair of baby blue hospital pants that hung loosely on my thinning waist. My long golden brown hair was oily and I hadn't seen my reflection in weeks.

The nurse escorted a group of us into the hospital chapel for a time of reflection. I sat on the cold, wooden pew and bowed my head in a sign of desperation. I began to mumble prayers to God, asking for His help to rebuild my life from the wreckage. Suddenly, the most beautiful melody filled the little room as a woman in my ward of the hospital began to sing "Amazing Grace."

Amazing grace! how sweet the sound
That saved a wretch like me!
I once was lost, but now am found;
Was blind, but now I see.[1]

The presence of God overwhelmed me. I sensed the Holy Spirit and came undone as the first tears I had cried in months streamed down my face. I felt God calling me to live, inviting me to follow Him and become brand new. In that moment through a whispered prayer, I turned away from my way of living and surrendered my life to Jesus Christ. That was the day I began to live fully alive. I've never been the same.

> **I felt God calling me to live, inviting me to follow Him and become brand new. . . . I've never been the same.**

As our time on this journey toward finding the identity, love, and worth we are created for comes to a close, I hope you will show grace to yourself. I hope you will be kind to yourself as you seek to grow in God and live out the life you've been made for. God does not expect you to live into your true purpose perfectly or immediately. Instead, He just invites you to follow Him day by day as He gently shows you the path to life and the fullness of joy. He is there any time you slip or want to go the other way. You cannot outrun His grace.

I hope you are finding answers to the big questions you have about your place in this world—about why you're here, who God really is, and what is ahead for you. I hope the lies in your head are getting quieter as the voice of truth invites you to be still and be loved. I pray you believe in the core of your being that you are truly wonderfully made—made with love and dignity for such a time as this. I hope you know you play an irreplaceable role in God's great story, a story that ends in victory. I hope you believe that you are a pearl of great price, forgiven, renewed, and free.

I have discovered my best, joy-filled life is hidden in God. In Christ, I am fully alive. I'm dead to my shortcomings and bad decisions, even though I still miss the mark. I am alive in a grace so radical it loves me at my darkest, but refuses to let me stay there. This love can't be earned by hustle, success, beauty, or influence. It is a gift I can only receive through faith.

Living fully alive doesn't mean never experiencing pain, suffering, or grief. As I look back at the worst moments of my life, I realize that even when I felt dead inside, I was fully alive because God was in me, fighting my battles: "You, dear children, are from God and have overcome them [evil spirits], because the one who is in you is greater than the one who is in the world" (1 John 4:4). His eternal plan for me has always been good. This is true for you as well.

The sparkle of the world can turn our gaze from the light of God. God is often misunderstood, disregarded, and shut out of the world He made. As women who live in the light, we are called to go to those in the dark and tell them how great the Father's love is. Let our lives be a living prayer. Let us live a good story that tells of a great God.

Jesus teaches us how to live fully alive: "As the Father has loved me, so have I loved you. Now remain in my love" (John 15:9). We are to be established and rooted in His love—to live so loved that it defines who we are. To remain in God's love is to know that is where you find your identity, worth, and purpose. Living fully alive means living into your true God-given identity as His redeemed, chosen, forgiven, and loved daughter. There is nothing you can do to add to your worth or take away from it. It is securely established as a child of God.

Jesus continues, "If you keep my commands, you will remain in my love, just as I have kept my Father's commands and remain in his love. I have told you this so that my joy may be in you and that your joy may be complete" (John 15:10–11). To live a joy-filled life—to live our best life—we are to walk in obedience. Obedience might sound constrictive or boring, but living for God is the most beautiful adventure. His way of life keeps us safe from unnecessary destruction, ultimately making us happier. We are most alive when we are walking in God's precepts, which keeps us joyful and free.

To live fully alive is to love others well.

Jesus teaches, "My command is this: Love each other as I have loved you" (John 15:12). This is a command to live with an outward focus. We are called to be women who know our worth and have self-love but are not lovers of ourselves. We are called to be women who cherish those the world has forgotten. We see past our reflection to the needs of others. We make others feel significant. In our presence, friends, family, and strangers experience God's love.

To be fully alive is to be near to God.

We are invited to a friendship with God. Jesus continues,

"Greater love has no one than this: to lay down one's life for one's friends. You are my friends if you do what I command. I no longer call you servants, because a servant does not know his master's business. Instead, I have called you friends, for everything that I learned from my Father I have made known to you." (John 15:13–15)

God desires this friendship with you to be an intimate, ongoing relationship.

Finding your identity is also about knowing you have been chosen. Jesus says,

"You did not choose me, but I chose you and appointed you so that you might go and bear fruit—fruit that will last—and so that whatever you ask in my name the Father will give you. This is my command: Love each other." (John 15:16–17)

This abundant life creates beauty and goodness and points others to God.

To live fully alive is to live loved.

It's knowing your value. It's believing you have been made with intention and purpose. It's walking in grace, not perfection. It's being separate from the darkness and a lover of the light and all that is good, lovely, and true. It's turning your back on the wide road of the world and setting your feet firmly on the narrow path that leads to an abundant life, no matter how unpopular it may be. It's taking up your cross and doing the hard things, knowing God's strength is made perfect in weakness. It's laying your life down to find the life you were made for. It's leaving this world more in awe of God and living life to the fullest because in Christ you are fully alive. May you know that you are wonderfully made and live loved, whole, and free. In God, your best life is waiting for you.

Be Still and Be Loved

A TIME TO REFLECT

What does living fully alive mean to you?

God,
Thank You for loving and rescuing me. Teach me the abundant life You desire for me. Help me to live loved and live fully alive in You.

Appendix

Father's Love Letter[1]

My Child,

You may not know me, but I know everything about you.
PSALM 139:1

I know when you sit down and when you rise up.
PSALM 139:2

I am familiar with all your ways.
PSALM 139:3

Even the very hairs on your head are numbered.
MATTHEW 10:29–31

For you were made in my image.
GENESIS 1:27

In me you live and move and have your being.
ACTS 17:28

For you are my offspring.
ACTS 17:28

I knew you even before you were conceived.
JEREMIAH 1:4–5

I chose you when I planned creation.

EPHESIANS 1:11–12

You were not a mistake, for all your days are written in my book.

PSALM 139:15–16

I determined the exact time of your birth and where you would live.

ACTS 17:26

You are fearfully and wonderfully made.

PSALM 139:14

I knit you together in your mother's womb.

PSALM 139:13

And brought you forth on the day you were born.

PSALM 71:6

I have been misrepresented by those who don't know me.

JOHN 8:41–44

I am not distant and angry, but am the complete expression of love.

1 JOHN 4:16

And it is my desire to lavish my love on you.

1 JOHN 3:1

Simply because you are my child and I am your Father.

1 JOHN 3:1

I offer you more than your earthly father ever could.

MATTHEW 7:11

For I am the perfect father.

MATTHEW 5:48

Every good gift that you receive comes from my hand.

JAMES 1:17

For I am your provider and I meet all your needs.

MATTHEW 6:31–33

My plan for your future has always been filled with hope.

JEREMIAH 29:11

Because I love you with an everlasting love.

JEREMIAH 31:3

My thoughts toward you are countless as the sand on the seashore.

PSALM 139:17–18

And I rejoice over you with singing.

ZEPHANIAH 3:17

I will never stop doing good to you.

JEREMIAH 32:40

For you are my treasured possession.

EXODUS 19:5

I desire to establish you with all my heart and all my soul.

JEREMIAH 32:41

And I want to show you great and marvelous things.

JEREMIAH 33:3

If you seek me with all your heart, you will find me.

DEUTERONOMY 4:29

Delight in me and I will give you the desires of your heart.

PSALM 37:4

For it is I who gave you those desires.

PHILIPPIANS 2:13

I am able to do more for you than you could possibly imagine.

EPHESIANS 3:20

For I am your greatest encourager.

2 THESSALONIANS 2:16–17

I am also the Father who comforts you in all your troubles.

2 CORINTHIANS 1:3–4

When you are brokenhearted, I am close to you.

PSALM 34:18

As a shepherd carries a lamb, I have carried you close to
my heart.

ISAIAH 40:11

One day I will wipe away every tear from your eyes.

REVELATION 21:3–4

And I'll take away all the pain you have suffered on this earth.

REVELATION 21:3–4

I am your Father, and I love you even as I love my son, Jesus.

JOHN 17:23

For in Jesus, my love for you is revealed.

JOHN 17:26

He is the exact representation of my being.

HEBREWS 1:3

He came to demonstrate that I am for you, not against you.

ROMANS 8:31

And to tell you that I am not counting your sins.

2 CORINTHIANS 5:18–19

Jesus died so that you and I could be reconciled.

2 CORINTHIANS 5:18–19

His death was the ultimate expression of my love for you.

1 JOHN 4:10

I gave up everything I loved that I might gain your love.

ROMANS 8:31–32

If you receive the gift of my son Jesus, you receive me.

1 JOHN 2:23

And nothing will ever separate you from my love again.

ROMANS 8:38–39

Come home and I'll throw the biggest party heaven has ever seen.

LUKE 15:7

I have always been Father, and will always be Father.

EPHESIANS 3:14–15

My question is . . . Will you be my child?
JOHN 1:12–13

I am waiting for you.
LUKE 15:11–32

Love, Your Dad

Almighty God

An Invitation to Give Your Life to God

Give God your life and let Him give you an identity, purpose, and worth that lasts forever. Use this prayer as a guide to surrender your heart and life to Jesus.

Dear God,

I need You. Thank You that You love me and came to this world to save me. I confess that I am guilty of sin and living in a way that separates me from You. I ask that You forgive me and renew my heart and life with Your presence.

Jesus, I believe you are Lord, that You conquered death and that nothing will ever separate me from Your love. I am placing my trust in You alone, and I accept Your gift of eternal life. Thank You for calling me Your child. I give You my life.

If you have prayed this for the first time to give your life to Christ, feel free to sign your name and the date of your decision. Now share this awesome news with someone.

Signature _____

Date _____

Book Club Questions

Hey, Friend! I am so glad you are journeying through this book with others, and I hope you experience joy and community through your time together. Below are suggested questions you can use to discuss what you've read. Feel free to just pick your favorite questions, or if you have time, tackle them all. I recommend discussing five chapters each week for six weeks (so maybe one question per week, depending on your group's size). But you have the freedom to do what works best for your group. Commit to holding what is shared in confidentiality as you grow with others.

WEEK 1

1. Made by God

Describe the most beautiful place you have ever been.

What do you experience when you gaze at the beauty of creation?

How do you think what you believe about how you came into existence influences your sense of identity and purpose?

2. Made to Know God

What is your impression of the Bible?

How can you allow the Bible's wisdom to transform your life?

What verses have had a profound impact on your life? Please share some of them with one another.

3. Made for a Relationship with God

Share about the first time you remember hearing about Jesus.

Do you believe Jesus was a liar, lunatic, or Lord? Why so?

How does what you believe about Jesus influence your life?

4. Made in the Image of God

What does it mean to you to be made in God's image?

How does the truth that you bear God's image influence the way you see yourself?

What does it look like to be an image bearer of God to a world desperate for love and truth?

5. Made with Love and Wonder

Do you ever have a hard time believing your value? If so, why do you think that is?

What does being wonderfully made mean to you?

How can you praise God with your life and take Him at His word when He says you have been fearfully or lovingly and wonderfully made?

WEEK 2

6. Made to Glorify God

Whose glory do you think most people in our culture are living for? Their own or God's?

What does it mean to give God the spotlight in your life?

How can you glorify God through the gifts, passions, and talents He's given you?

7. **Made to Bloom**

If your life is a garden, what does it look like?

What are some weeds in your life that might be keeping you from truly blooming?

How can you bloom and flourish right where God has you in this season?

8. **Made for Beauty**

What does it look like to build a life on one's outward appearance?

How can you cultivate a beauty that never fades?

Share about a woman in your life who makes you feel valued, loved, and known.

9. **Made for Something More**

What does it mean to you that you have been made for more?

What are you clinging on to when God might have something better in store for you?

What worthless things are keeping you from living a life of deep purpose and significance?

10. **Made to Live Forever**

What does it mean to you to "number your days"?

How can you live a life of purpose on earth while keeping a heavenly perspective?

What most excites you about heaven?

WEEK 3

11. Made to Live Fearlessly

What are your greatest fears and anxieties and what would it look like to entrust them to God?

What practical tools and strategies shared in the chapter can you implement in your life to ease anxiety and fear?

What negative influences in your life might be intensifying your fear or anxiety?

12. Made to Walk Worthy

How do you understand shame and have you ever experienced it?

How can you allow God to be the lifter of your shame?

What things do you need to stop listening to and looking to so you can experience freedom from shame and inadequacy?

13. Made to Be Redeemed

What in your life needs God's mending or redemption?

How can you surrender the broken parts of your life to Christ?

Have you ever found unexpected gifts from some of the hard things in your life?

14. Made to Belong

How can the truth that you belong to God give you peace and security?

Where do you feel most loved and accepted?

Where can you experience deeper belonging and how can you create space for others to belong?

15. Made for Friendship

Are your friendships bringing you closer to God or further apart?

What does true friendship look like to you?

Have you ever worked through a changing friendship? What did you learn?

WEEK 4

16. Made to Persevere

Has suffering been a part of your story?

What do you think of the concept that we all have an invisible wheelchair?

How can you fight for joy in seasons of pain and struggle?

17. Made for Such a Time as This

What does it mean to you that you have been made for "such a time as this"?

Where does your "deep gladness and the world's deep hunger" meet?

Do you have a clear sense of calling on your life, or are you praying for clarity and direction?

18. Made for Soul Care

Why do you think women can sometimes have a hard time treating themselves with kindness and respect?

What are some ways you would like to practice better soul care?

What is one life-giving habit, routine, or discipline you can start implementing into your life?

19. Made to Create

What do you feel called to create?

Have comparison and distraction ever kept you from creating?

How can you live a quieter life of deep presence and contentment?

20. Made for Forgiveness

How have you experienced forgiveness?

What is the hardest part about forgiving someone who has wronged you?

How does the act of forgiving someone influence you personally?

WEEK 5

21. Made for Sexual Wholeness

What are some of the lies about sexuality our world pushes on girls and women?

Why do you think there is so much sexual brokenness in our world?

What does it look like to pursue a life of sexual integrity in today's culture?

22. **Made to Live Wisely**

How does it feel to have so much freedom to make
your own decisions?

What does it mean to you to live wisely?

In what areas of your life do you need more wisdom?

23. **Made to Be Present**

Do you feel engaged with or detached from your actual life?

What negative effects do you think social media
is having on us?

What are some tangible things you can do to help
you practice the spiritual discipline of presence?

24. **Made to Rest**

Is a day of rest a part of your week?

What restores your soul?

What are some practical ways you can incorporate rhythms of
rest and renewal into both your daily life and
one set-apart day a week?

25. **Made for an Outward-Focused Life**

Why do you think it can be so easy to be self-focused?

How does insecurity or pride manifest in our lives?

How can you make the people in your life feel valued?

WEEK 6

26. Made for a Mission

Who has God placed in your life that you feel called to share God's love with?

How can you be ready to give a clear explanation of the hope that is inside you?

Where do you sense God sending you?

27. Made to Be Faithful

What are some things God has entrusted you with?

What is God calling you to be faithful with?

What does it mean to you to live a faithful life?

28. Made to Be Transformed

What are you believing about God, yourself, and your future that is untrue, and how can you renew your mind?

What is one verse you can commit to memory?

How can you cultivate a spirit of gratitude?

29. Made to Worship

What do you think of when you hear the word "worship"?

What expression of worship is a part of your life now?

What would it look like to live fully surrendered to God?

30. **Made to Live Fully Alive**

What does living fully alive mean to you?

What does it look like to walk in your true identity, purpose, and worth?

How can you cultivate a deeper friendship with God?

Getting Outside Help

You make this world a more beautiful place, and we need you here. If you are struggling with suicidal thoughts, please tell someone you can trust and call this number:

Suicide Hotline
800-273-8255

If you have experienced sexual assault or rape, reach out for help.

Sexual Assault Hotline
1-800-656-4673

Acknowledgments

Paul, thank you for being my constant sunshine, my faithful partner, and my dream come true. I am forever grateful for the way you daily make me laugh out loud and encourage me to pursue the dreams God has put in my heart.

Dad, thanks for being my editor in chief. You are my rock and hero and are "oftentimes" . . . okay, always . . . right.

Mom, you have paved the road for me to chase my dreams and catch them. Thanks for showing me what is possible with kindness and hard work.

To Dave Schroeder, my "epic" agent! Thank you for surprising me in my inbox, believing in me, and helping make this book a reality. These words wouldn't exist without you. I am forever grateful. Here's to more to come!

Judy Dunagan, thank you for taking a chance on me, believing in this message, and giving me the honor to be one of Moody's authors. Amanda Cleary Eastep, thank you for refining my work and for your excellent attention to detail. Erik Peterson, you blew me away with this stunning cover design, full of beauty and depth. I'm grateful to the entire Moody team who helped bring this book to the world.

To every girl and woman who has ever been a part of Wonderfully Made for the past seventeen years (too many to name!)—this is for you! You inspire me to keep our mission alive. We will press on until every girl and woman knows the identity, love, and worth she was created for.

Notes

Introduction

1. Zach Hrynowski, "How Many Americans Believe in God?," Gallup, November 8, 2019, https://news.gallup.com/poll/268205/americans-believe-god.aspx.

1. Made by God

1. Plato, *The Apology of Socrates*, H. N. Fowler Translation, Loeb (1913), 25.

2. Lee Strobel, *The Case for a Creator: A Journalist Investigates Scientific Evidence That Points Toward God* (Grand Rapids, MI: Zondervan, 2004), 77–78.

3. Lee Strobel, Twitter, tweet referring to his quote in *Case for a Creator*, December 24, 2017.

4. John Templeton, *The Humble Approach: Scientists Discover God* (Radnor, PA: Templeton Foundation Press, 1995), 19.

2. Made to Know God

1. St. Augustine of Hippo, *Enarrationes*, Psalter xc, sermon 2, 354–430.

3. Made for a Relationship with God

1. C. S. Lewis, *Mere Christianity* (San Francisco: HarperOne, revised and expanded edition, 2015), 52 (emphasis added).

2. William Angus Knight, *Colloquia Peripatetica: Deep-Sea Soundings: Being Notes of Conversations with the Late John Duncan, LL. D., Professor of Hebrew in the New College* (Edinburgh: David Douglas, 1879), 109.

3. Brennan Manning, *Abba's Child: The Cry of the Heart for Intimate Belonging* (Colorado Springs: NavPress, 2015), 35.

4. Ibid., 42.

4. Made in the Image of God

1. Paul Brand and Philip Yancey, *Fearfully and Wonderfully Made* (Downers Grove, IL: IVP Books, 2019), 13.

5. Made with Love and Wonder

1. Strong's H3372, Blue Letter Bible, https://www.blueletterbible.org/lexicon/h3372/kjv/wlc/0-1/.

2. Lexico, s.v. "wonderful," https://www.lexico.com/en/definition/wonderful.

3. Tracy D. Wade, Anna Keski-Rahkonen, and James I. Hudson, "The Epidemiology of Eating Disorders," in *Textbook of Psychiatric Epidemiology*, Ming T. Tsuang, Mauricio Tohen, and Peter B. Jones, eds. (Hoboken, NJ: John Wiley & Sons, 2011), 343–60.

4. Author interview with Angela Rodgers, *Wonderfully Made* podcast, September 30, 2019.

6. Made to Glorify God

1. *Merriam Webster*, s.v. "self-actualize," https://www.merriam-webster.com/dictionary/self-actualize.

2. "The Westminster Shorter Catechism," completed in 1647 by the Westminster Assembly, Question 1, https://www.apuritansmind.com/westminster-standards/shorter-catechism.

3. "What Does It Mean to Glorify God?," GotQuestions.org, last updated April 26, 2021, https://www.gotquestions.org/glorify-God.html.

4. John Piper, "Glorifying God . . . Period," Desiring God, Campus Outreach Staff Conference, Orlando, FL, July 15, 2013, https://www.desiringgod.org/messages/glorifying-god-period.

5. John Piper, "God Is Most Glorified in Us When We Are Most Satisfied in Him," Desiring God, October 13, 2012, https://www.desiringgod.org/messages/god-is-most-glorified-in-us-when-we-are-most-satisfied-in-him.

6. Bethany Hamilton, Sheryl Berk, and Rick Bundschuh, *Soul Surfer: A True Story of Faith, Family, and Fighting to Get Back on the Board* (New York: Pocket Books, 2004), 159.

7. Ibid., 140.

8. Made for Beauty

1. John and Stasi Eldredge, *Captivating: Unveiling the Mystery of a Woman's Soul* (Nashville: Thomas Nelson, 2010), 27.

9. Made for Something More

1. Attributed to Ann Voskamp.

10. Made to Live Forever

1. C. S. Lewis, *Mere Christianity* (San Francisco: HarperOne, Revised & Enlarged edition, 2015), 136.

2. Randy Alcorn, *Heaven: A Comprehensive Guide to Everything the Bible Says About Our Eternal Home* (Carol Stream, IL: Tyndale, 2004), 28.

3. Will L. Thompson, "Eternity," public domain, https://www.hymnsuntogod
.org/Hymns-PD/E-Hymns/Eternity.html.

11. Made to Live Fearlessly

1. Frederick Buechner, *Beyond Words: Daily Readings in the ABC's of Faith* (New York: HarperCollins, 2004), 139.

13. Made to Be Redeemed

1. Collins Dictionary, s.v. "Kintsugi," New Word Suggestion, https://www
.collinsdictionary.com/us/submission/19460/Kintsugi.

2. Lexico, s.v. "redemption," https://www.lexico.com/en/definition/redemption.

16. Made to Persevere

1. Interview with Katherine Wolf, *Wonderfully Made* podcast, August 17, 2020.

2. "Embrace the Life God Has Given You, Two Minute Clip on Grief" (video), Desiring God, November 28, 2020, https://www.desiringgod.org/ embrace-the-life-god-has-given-you.

17. Made for Such a Time as This

1. Rosa Parks, *Quiet Strength: The Faith, the Hope, and the Heart of a Woman Who Changed a Nation* (Grand Rapids, MI: Zondervan, 1994), 17–18.

2. Frederick Buechner, *Wishful Thinking: A Theological ABC* (San Francisco: Harper & Row, 1990), 118–19.

18. Made for Soul Care

1. Mental Health Disorder Statistics, https://www.hopkinsmedicine.org/ health/wellness-and-prevention/mental-health-disorder-statistics.

19. Made to Create

1. Panel interview featuring Morgan Harper Nichols, Anchored in Love Conference, October 26, 2019.

20. Made for Forgiveness

1. Corrie ten Boom, with Jamie Buckingham, *Tramp for the Lord* (Fort Washington, PA: CLC Publications, 1974), 55.

2. Ibid., 56.

3. Ibid., 57.

4. Ibid.

5. C. S. Lewis, *Mere Christianity* (San Francisco: HarperOne, Revised & Enlarged edition, 2015), 115.

21. Made for Sexual Wholeness

1. Karen Mizoguchi, "Miley Cyrus: 'I Am Open to Every Single Thing That Is Consenting and Doesn't Involve an Animal,'" August 12, 2019, https://www.nme.com/news/music/miley-cyrus-33-1209000.

23. Made to Be Present

1. "10-year study shows elevated suicide risk from excess social media time for teen girls," *Newswise*, February 9, 2021, https://www.newswise.com/articles/10-year-study-shows-elevated-suicide-risk-from-excess-social-media-time-for-teen-girls.

2. Henri Nouwen, *Love, Henri: Letters on the Spiritual Life* (New York: Convergent Books, First Edition, October 4, 2016), 112.

3. Kate Merrick, *Here, Now: Unearthing Peace and Presence in an Overconnected World* (Nashville, TN: Nelson Books, 2019), 13.

24. Made to Rest

1. Rhett Power, "A Day of Rest: 12 Scientific Reasons It Works," January 1, 2017, https://www.inc.com.

25. Made for an Outward-Focused Life

1. Stendhal, *The Red and the Black: A Chronicle of the Nineteenth Century* (New York: Oxford University Press, 1998), 409.

2. Often mistakenly attributed to C. S. Lewis, the author is unknown but a variation is attributed to Ken Blanchard, author of *One Minute Manager*, who is quoted as saying, "Don't think less of yourself, just think of yourself less," https://checkyourfact.com/2019/06/30/fact-check-cs-lewis-mere-christianity-humility-thinking-less-yourself.

3. Timothy Keller, *The Freedom of Self-Forgetfulness: The Path to True Christian Joy* (Farington, UK: 10Publishing, 2012), 33.

28. Made to Be Transformed

1. "CBT's Cognitive Restructuring (CR) for Tackling Cognitive Distortions," PositivePsychology.com, October 13, 2020, https://positivepsychology.com/cbt-cognitive-restructuring-cognitive-distortions.

2. Courtney E. Ackerman, "What Is Neuroplasticity? A Psychologist Explains," Positivepsychology.com, December 10, 2020, https://positivepsychology.com/neuroplasticity.

29. Made to Worship

1. John Piper, *Let the Nations Be Glad: The Supremacy of God in Missions* (Grand Rapids, MI: Baker Academic, 2010), 231.

2. "Worship," YouVersion Events, Stone's Hill Community Church, https://www.bible.com/events/275580.

3. Lexico, s.v. "worthship," https://www.lexico.com/en/definition/worthship.

4. Helen H. Lemmel, "Turn Your Eyes Upon Jesus," 1922, Public Domain.

30. Made to Live Fully Alive

1. John V. Newton, "Amazing Grace," hymn, 1789, public domain.

Appendix

1. "Father's Love Letter," © 1999 Father Heart Communications, www.FathersLoveLetter.com. Used with permission.

Join our Community

wonderfullymade.org

RESOURCES, ENCOURAGEMENT & MORE!

Wonderfully Made® is a 501(c)(3) nonprofit organization dedicated to helping teen girls and young women know their God-given value, while encouraging and equipping them to live spiritually and emotionally healthy lives.

POST A PIC

of your copy of *Wonderfully Made* and share it with us on Instagram @wonderfullymade_org or tell us how this book impacted you and write us at info@wonderfullymade.org. Thanks so much for reading!

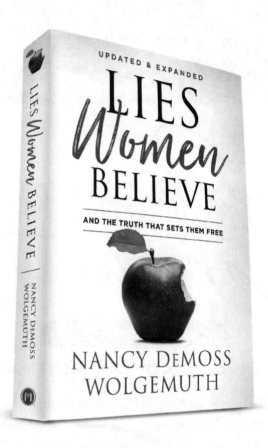

Encounter the fullness of God's grace, the power of His promises, and the beauty of His faithfulness—all through the life of one woman: Esther.

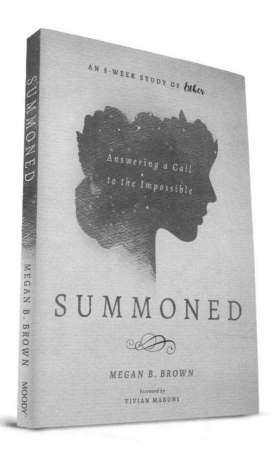

In *Summoned*, you'll enter the story of Esther—her calling, pain, and role in God's plan for salvation—and see how God is always working in the lives of His people, even when He seems distant. Through this 8-week study, you'll develop a deeper appreciation for God's Word and begin to see that stepping out in faith for His glory is often the first step to encountering His redeeming love.

978-0-8024-2169-2 | also available as an eBook

Do you feel that hearing God's voice is for others
but not you? Is it only for people who
lived in biblical times?